HERE'S WHAT PEOPLE ⟩
BRADLEY TRUMAN NOEL AND
TINDER, TATTOOS, AND TEQUILA...

This accessible volume welcomes us to join in more fully on conversations we are already having (or should be!) in the church. Bradley Noel offers poignant and practical direction along the way toward thinking biblically and theologically about many of the very matters that actually matter to the church today, and he does so with his usual wit and humor, insight and understanding.

—*Dr. Rick Wadholm Jr.*
Associate Professor of Old Testament
Assemblies of God Theological Seminary, Springfield, MO

My colleague and friend, Dr. Bradley Noel, takes on a very practical examination of a centuries-long challenge that those who follow Jesus Christ have wrestled with. How do we become like the Holy One without losing our way into the excesses of legalism or license? In *Tinder, Tattoos, and Tequila,* Brad engages the historic tension between law and grace. The goal is that the reader ends up looking more like Jesus rather than a task-driven keeper of a code.

To achieve this goal, the author provides a widely applicable tool of five questions that the reader can engage as they address the various situations and decisions they make in life. These questions are addressed in a systematic, winsome, and consistently applicable manner. At a time when polarized thinking seems to rule the day, this book's wise approach to living out gracious truth in everyday life is a highly valued resource for those who would be like Jesus and fulfill His mission.

—*Rev. David Wells*
General Superintendent, Pentecostal Assemblies of Canada
Vice-Chair, Pentecostal World Fellowship

Knowing how to navigate moral decisions is more difficult than ever for Christians, especially when they don't always agree on what's the right or wrong thing to do! Dr. Bradley Noel provides a way forward, challenging both the legalist and libertarian to embrace a more biblical way of navigating the "gray" areas of morality. Drawing on years of experience as both a pastor and a theologian, Noel avoids a simplistic approach to resolving the "disputable matters" on which Christians may hold strong and yet opposing convictions, such as alcohol, tattoos, or even social media. Instead, he proposes a series of five questions aimed to guide the believer in discerning the direction of the Holy Spirit. Using real-life illustrations and humor, Noel engages the reader and imparts scriptural truth and practical wisdom, with the goal of forming disciples who are mature in their ability to make godly decisions in a complex world. *Tinder, Tattoos, and Tequila* would especially serve as a valuable guidebook for Christian youth and young adults.

—*Dr. Peter Neumann*
Academic Dean, Master's College and Seminary, Peterborough, Ontario

BRADLEY TRUMAN NOEL

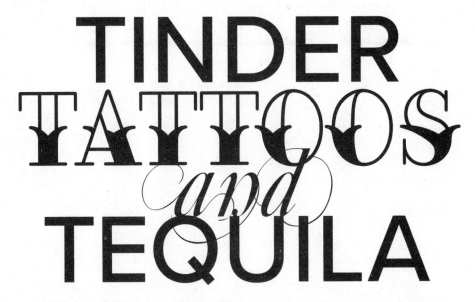

TINDER
TATTOOS
and
TEQUILA

NAVIGATING THE GRAY AREAS OF FAITH

WHITAKER
HOUSE

TINDER, TATTOOS, AND TEQUILA
Navigating the Gray Areas of Faith

www.youtube.com/channel/UCVTd6yJ6n7eYcLaSrO9O0wQ
twitter.com/bradley_noel
www.facebook.com/bradley.t.noel

ISBN: 978-1-64123-830-4
eBook ISBN: 978-1-64123-831-1

Printed in the United States of America
© 2022 by Bradley Truman Noel

Whitaker House
1030 Hunt Valley Circle
New Kensington, PA 15068
www.whitakerhouse.com

Library of Congress Cataloging-in-Publication Data (Pending)

1 2 3 4 5 6 7 8 9 10 11 ⨄ 29 28 27 26 25 24 23 22

DEDICATION

For Melinda
in our twenty-fifth year of marriage:
Celebrating with you the completion of your
Doctorate of Medicine.
You are a model of compassion, generosity, and perseverance.
I could not be more proud.

CONTENTS

ACKNOWLEDGMENTS

Deepest appreciation to the many youth groups, camps, chapels, and online audiences that have heard me teach on this topic over the last twenty years. Your questions and comments have made this work immeasurably stronger.

I recall with great fondness my youth group in Springdale from 1999–2001, the aptly named Xplosion Youth Ministry. I served there with a youth executive team that was far and away better than I could have hoped for, and from whom I learned so much. The first four questions used in this book came from my interactions with them.

Special thanks to my friend Mike Miller. Having taught on wisdom one day at our youth convention, he inspired me to add the fifth question to the list.

For decades, Melinda and I have been privileged to count Lorne and Cathy Robinson as friends in the truest sense of the word. With them, we have mourned and celebrated, ranted and laughed. My conversations with Lorne as a young man particularly shaped who I am today. Cathy kindly read a draft of this manuscript and made a number of excellent suggestions that found their way into the copy you're reading.

Thanks to David Wells, Peter Neumann, and Rick Wadholm Jr. for taking the time to read a draft of this book, showing such generosity with your time and graciousness in your endorsements.

I owe Don Milam, Peg Fallon, Christine Whitaker, and the rest of the team at Whitaker House a debt of gratitude. It's been a pleasure partnering with you on this endeavor! I so appreciate the sense of calling and excellence that you've demonstrated throughout this project.

I have such fondness for my students at Tyndale, where I'm privileged to serve, particularly those graduates who have now become some of our dearest friends. I draw daily encouragement and motivation from your love and example.

As always, my deepest love and gratitude are reserved for Melinda, who continues to be such an inspiration to me and so many others.

Soli Deo Gloria.

—*Bradley Truman Noel*
Springdale, Newfoundland, Canada
Third Sunday After Epiphany, 2022

INTRODUCTION

Whether you're reading this of your own free will, because you were coerced as part of a church group, or because your mother-in-law insisted you do so, I'm so glad you've picked up this book! I'm pleased because I believe this is going to be helpful to you as you seek to live your best life for God in the midst of what are some *really* interesting times.

Why a title like *Tinder, Tattoos, and Tequila*, you may ask? Excellent question. Well, I've long been convinced that the church has been plagued by two extremes when it comes to living a Christian lifestyle.

On one side, we have the serious folks adorned with really impressive frowns, who remind us of all the *do's and don'ts*. (To be honest, the list of things we're not allowed to do always seems to be much more extensive than the list of things that make God happy!) So Christianity—our faith in Jesus—gets reduced to a list of things we may or may not do. Our Christian walk resembles a course in legal proceedings, where a great many things are illegal and punishable in court, so we must carefully avoid them in the hopes of staying out of jail—or, rather, hell. If you're thinking, "Wow, that doesn't seem like much fun," you'd be absolutely correct. Long known as *legalism* within the church, this approach has sadly been the go-to path toward holiness for a great many Christian denominations over centuries past, and it is still the case for some today.

On the other end of the spectrum, however, are the folks who seem to be much happier. Their frown has been turned upside down. They aren't quite so burdened down with all of the rules and regulations that their brothers and sisters across the way struggle with. No indeed. They don't view the Christian life in legal terms at all. Rather, in a misunderstanding of what we call the *grace of God*, these folks play fast and loose with the rules. Their attitude is, "If God's grace covers our sin, then why worry? If God forgives every sin, let's live our best lives now!" These believers typically don't spend too much time thinking about holiness, or wondering if their actions align with biblical teaching on the choices and actions of the believer. They live by a mantra oft described by the more legalistic folks as "anything goes."

Unfortunately, neither of these all-too-common approaches to holiness really captures what the Bible teaches in terms of how we should live our lives. The *legalistic* folks miss the power of God's grace in our lives. Incidentally, the *anything-goes* folks miss the power of God's grace as well! Grace is simply that important. So before we go any further, let's figure out what we mean when we use these words and make sure that we're all on the same page. (Pun fully intended ☺.)

WHAT IS HOLINESS, ANYWAY?

When we talk about *holiness*, we're using an English word that comes from words in Hebrew (the language of the Old Testament) and Greek (the language of the New Testament) that mean "to be set apart." In the Bible, things could be set apart for God's use. For example, the gold, silver, and utensils destined for the temple were dedicated for the use of God alone. (See 1 Kings 15:15.) But more importantly, the people of God were set apart. God told the Israelites quite plainly:

> *You must be holy because I, the LORD, am holy. I have **set you apart** from all other people to be my very own.*   (Leviticus 20:26 NLT)

This theme is then carried forward into the New Testament. Holiness doesn't become any less important now that we live under grace and are no longer trying to fulfill the law of the Old Testament. In fact, quoting Leviticus, Peter writes:

> *But now **you must be holy** in everything you do, just as God who chose you is holy. For the Scriptures say, "You must be holy because I am holy."*   (1 Peter 1:15–16 NLT)

Hebrews 12:14 actually tells us that without holiness, no one will see the Lord! So, we are to be set apart for God in everything we do: our choices, our conduct, our words, and even our thoughts. It's a tall order! But happily, as we'll see later in this book, we have some incredible help—in fact, the very best help possible.

GOD'S MARVELOUS GRACE

When we talk about *God's grace*, we're really talking about unmerited favor; that is, God bestows His favor on us even though we don't deserve it. God's grace is like getting a gift that you don't deserve, not just once but repeatedly. (God's mercy, on the other hand, is quite similar, but in the opposite direction: God is merciful in that we *don't get* what we *do* deserve, which is punishment!) The Bible teaches that our salvation itself is made possible by the grace of God:

> **God saved you by his grace** *when you believed. And you can't take credit for this; it is a gift from God. Salvation is not a reward for the good things we have done, so none of us can boast about it.*
>
> (Ephesians 2:8–9 NLT)

Did you catch that? It's by grace that we've been saved. It's not something that we can earn, no matter how hard we try, or how closely we follow the teaching of Scripture. It just can't be earned. Why? So that none of us can boast about how well we've done, or how many good works we've accomplished. No, it's the free gift of God to undeserving people. That's the grace of God.

Now, it turns out that this undeserved favor, the grace of God, also helps us when it comes to holiness. A passage from Paul's letter to Titus is worth reading here, as it clearly links the grace we've been given and the holy lives we're to lead:

> *For **the grace of God has appeared** that offers salvation to all people. **It teaches us** to say "No" to ungodliness and worldly passions, and to live self-controlled, upright and godly lives in this present age, while we wait for the blessed hope—the appearing of the glory of our great God and Savior, Jesus Christ, who gave himself for us to redeem us from all wickedness and to purify for himself a people that are his very own, **eager to do what is good.*** (Titus 2:11–14)

And just like that, we're taught a couple of very important things about holiness, or being set apart for God.

First, the grace of God teaches us to live godly lives. We'll walk through how that happens in a later chapter. Second, and also very important, we read that while we live our lives, waiting for Jesus' return to earth, holiness is something that *we should be eager to do.* It's not the dreary legalism of rules and regulations, nor is it the careless attitude of living how we wish. Rather, because we're so grateful for God's free gift of salvation, and so thankful that God daily grants us undeserved favor, we gladly seek to offer our whole lives—thoughts, attitudes, decisions, and actions—back to Him for His glory.

BACK TO HOLINESS

Therefore, holiness happens in two stages, as it were. We are *set apart* for God at salvation and *are being set apart* as we grow in grace and holiness. Having been set apart for God when we accepted Jesus as Savior and Lord, we then continue to grow in grace and holiness for the rest of our Christian lives. Paul told the church at Corinth:

> *Because we have these promises, dear friends, let us cleanse ourselves from everything that can defile our body or spirit. And* **let us work toward complete holiness** *because we fear God.*
>
> (2 Corinthians 7:1 NLT)

And so the perfecting of holiness—our set-apartness—is a lifetime responsibility. My goal is to help you along the way. Holiness must be more than a lofty ideal; it must be a very practical undertaking, one that impacts our decisions on a daily basis. How exactly do we decide what things are good for us to do, and which ones dishonor God? It's one thing to be eager to do good, to be keen to grow in holiness, but it's quite another to make the good decisions that get us there! In starker terms, *how do we know what is sin and what isn't?*

HOW DO WE LIVE GODLY LIVES?

That's the question to which this book is dedicated. You'll learn how to make good decisions, enabling you to live a godly life, by understanding what things are wrong for us (sin) and what things are permissible.

Some things in Scripture are absolutes. They are commanded by God and apply to all believers, at all times, in all walks of life.

Other things, however, are not so clearly defined in the Bible. Should we use that latest app on our phones, or spend our money on the latest trends? The Bible certainly doesn't address TikTok in the letters of Paul! This book will give you the tools you need to walk through the gray areas of faith and culture, making decisions empowered by grace, and enabling you to strive for perfect holiness. But first, we must address those things that are simply not gray: the *absolutes*.

ABSOLUTELY ABSOLUTE

Absolutely not!" my father would declare, after I had asked permission for one thing or the other.

Given how emphatically he stated it and the accompanying glare, which was able to wither the hardiest of pleas (and plants!), I was left with little doubt as to the acceptance of my proposal! "Absolutely not" carries much more weight than a simple "No." Absolutes are firm and unchanging. In philosophy, an absolute is "a value or principle which is regarded as universally valid or which may be viewed without relation to other things...something that exists without being dependent on anything else."[1] My father's judgment was certainly universal as it

---

1. *Lexico*, s.v. "absolute," www.lexico.com/en/definition/absolute.

applied to our home and was not dependent on anything else, especially my opinion on the matter!

Before we can properly entertain a discussion on the gray areas of the faith, we must first pause and readily acknowledge that the Bible teaches us many absolutes. I will define *absolutes* as commands given by God that are applicable to all people everywhere, at all times, whether or not we agree, feel they're valid, or are inclined to obedience.

ABSOLUTES ARE COMMANDS GIVEN BY GOD THAT ARE APPLICABLE TO ALL PEOPLE EVERYWHERE, AT ALL TIMES, WHETHER OR NOT WE AGREE, FEEL THEY'RE VALID, OR ARE INCLINED TO OBEDIENCE.

So while some things in the Christian life are clearly gray, other things are plainly black and white, whether we like it or not. Before we proceed, let's take a few moments to consider some examples of absolutes in the Scriptures. This will help us better understand what gray areas are, and how we are to deal with them.

Now, when you hear talk of the *absolutes in Scripture*, your mind may go immediately to all of the "thou shalt nots," the infamous and widely lamented list of do's and don'ts.

As any purveyor of good Christian memes will quickly point out, following Jesus is not about *rules*; it's all about *relationship*. And that's true. Any honest student of Scripture will also tell you, however, that there are a number of commands in the Bible—the absolutes—that we must simply adhere to. But to turn the popular conception on its head, let's begin with a sample of those commands that are in the positive— things we *must* do, rather than things we are *forbidden* to do.

THE POSITIVE ABSOLUTES

FORGIVENESS

As it turns out, God commands us to do one of the things widely regarded by counselors and psychologists as essential to human mental health. We are to forgive, freely and without reservation. I realize that many people have been hurt, deeply and almost incomprehensively, all too often by someone they love, by believers in Christ, or by organizations that bear His name. I understand that forgetting what's been done to you is impossible. God understands that too. But He nonetheless calls us to forgive, for it sets our own minds, hearts, and even our bodies free from the hurt and bitterness that can so easily poison us. As Joyce Meyer once said, "Harboring unforgiveness is like drinking poison and hoping your enemy will die." Prolonged refusal to forgive simply does not end well for us, so God has insisted that we forgive others. For example, Paul wrote:

> *Be kind and compassionate to one another, forgiving each other, just as in Christ God forgave you.* (Ephesians 4:32)

Observing that we are to model God's own behavior toward us, Paul instructs us to treat one another with kindness and compassion. Would anyone argue that basic human kindness and compassion are not desperately needed in our world today? Although we are so *connected* via multiple forms of social media, we are simultaneously faced with a harshness and division that is so plainly insensitive in nature that it sometimes catches us off guard. Keyboard warriors—so named because they do their fighting remotely via their computers—say things to others that basic human decency would likely never allow them to say to another person face to face.

Further than kindness and compassion, Paul instructs us to forgive one another, just as God has forgiven us. Modelling the vertical relationship we have with Christ, we are to forgive horizontally those around us, in the same manner.

> *Bear with each other and forgive one another if any of you has a grievance against someone. Forgive as the Lord forgave you.*
>
> (Colossians 3:13)

Again, using the Lord as our model, Paul instructs us to bear with each other and forgive any grievances that arise in our daily interaction with others.

Matthew records some very helpful teaching on forgiveness from Jesus Himself:

> *Then Peter came to Jesus and asked, "Lord, how many times shall I forgive my brother or sister who sins against me? Up to seven times?" Jesus answered, "I tell you, not seven times, but seventy-seven times."*
>
> (Matthew 18:21–22)

According to some Bible translations, Jesus said we must forgive *"seventy times seven"* times—or four hundred and ninety times!

In this very well-known passage, Peter is earnestly inquiring about forgiveness. By now, the disciples probably sensed that Jesus was different than your average rabbi. His teachings certainly did not always toe the line of the local Pharisees and Sadducees. I imagine Peter was quite proud of his own question! He instinctively knew that Jesus would want him to forgive more than once, more than twice even. Some rabbis taught that forgiving someone three times was sufficient. So Peter really ups the ante! "Seven times, Lord? Surely that will cover it! You see, Lord, I'm getting your teaching; I'm catching the vision here. I know what this 'good news' is all about! So what about seven times? That'll do it, right?"

I can just imagine Jesus so patiently smiling, sensing what's in His disciple's heart. "No, Peter. 'A' for effort though. Not just seven times. Seventy times seven."

Can you see Peter's mouth fall open? Can you sense his astonishment? How is that even possible? Surely after 150 times, we're allowed to withhold forgiveness; by the 321st time, our adversary is *clearly* not learning the lesson our forgiveness is intended to teach! But that, of course, is not the Lord's point. As often as someone sins against us, we are to offer forgiveness. For all practical purposes, our forgiveness is supposed to be limitless.

Following Jesus' teaching in a passage now known as *The Lord's Prayer*—which includes the plea for forgiveness, *"And forgive us our debts, as we also have forgiven our debtors"* (Matthew 6:12)—Jesus makes a startling declaration:

> *For if you forgive other people when they sin against you, your heavenly Father will also forgive you. But if you do not forgive others their sins, your Father will not forgive your sins.*
>
> (Matthew 6:14–15)

Wow! What an *in-your-face* statement! It's hard to get much clearer than that when it comes to the incredible importance of forgiveness. Again, our ability to forgive others is taught in light of God's forgiveness of our own sins.

Now, on first reading, this teaching seems very difficult; is Jesus really saying that our *entire salvation* hinges on our ability to forgive others? If we are deeply harmed by someone, and it takes some years for us to fully process what they did or said and offer them forgiveness, is our eternal salvation hanging in the balance? Not at all.

New Testament scholar Leon Morris says it very well:

> It is not that the act of forgiving merits an eternal reward, but rather it is evidence that the grace of God is at work in the forgiving person and that that same grace will bring him forgiveness in due course. Forgiveness is important for the followers of Jesus, whereas the nature of the offenses committed against

them is not. Jesus is saying that to fail to forgive others is to demonstrate that one has not felt the saving touch of God.[2]

GIVING

Giving or tithing is a topic that many in the church *really* don't like! Many pastors avoid the topic (or so I hear) because their normal loving and encouraging congregation becomes quite, shall we say, quiet and even suspicious when the pastor begins talking about their wallets. Despite this, it is widely understood that Christians are to be a giving people. We are commanded to support the work of the kingdom. Paul teaches the Corinthians to put aside a sum of money in keeping with their income, to be given when they gather together. (See 1 Corinthians 16:2.) The church has long recognized that the command to give is for all believers, at all times, in all locations. As we know, this teaching first finds expression in the Old Testament:

> *"Will a mere mortal rob God? Yet you rob me. But you ask, 'How are we robbing you?' In tithes and offerings. You are under a curse— your whole nation—because you are robbing me. Bring the whole tithe into the storehouse, that there may be food in my house. Test me in this," says the* Lord *Almighty, "and see if I will not throw open the floodgates of heaven and pour out so much blessing that there will not be room enough to store it. I will prevent pests from devouring your crops, and the vines in your fields will not drop their fruit before it is ripe," says the* Lord *Almighty. "Then all the nations will call you blessed, for yours will be a delightful land," says the* Lord *Almighty.* (Malachi 3:8–12)

I don't think you have to be a biblical scholar to see that God is not altogether happy with His chosen people! It's hard to see how God could take giving, or the lack thereof, more seriously. He equates their

---

2. Leon Morris, *The Gospel According to Matthew, The Pillar New Testament Commentary* (Grand Rapids, MI; Leicester, England: W.B. Eerdmans; Inter-Varsity Press, 1992), 149.

failure to give with robbery. They are literally stealing from God, in His estimation. And let's face it, what other opinion counts?

One of the reasons that I find it so sad that this topic is often avoided is that it is inherently laden with good news! Yes, *giving* is a good news message! It's right there in that passage. After God chastises them for "*robbing*" Him of their tithes and offerings, He offers one of the greatest promises we could hope for. Despite the many times God tells us never to test Him, in this case, He's all about the test! God poses the challenge, "Give it a try! Give the proper tithes and offerings and just see if I won't '*throw open the floodgates of heaven and pour out so much blessing that there will not be room enough to store it*'!"

Can you imagine a challenge more wonderful than this?

How unfortunate it is, then, when believers can only see pastors who teach on giving as being after their money! Yes, God commands us to give—because inherent in our giving is His blessing upon us. We'll see more of this shortly in the New Testament. But further, I believe that God desires His children to give because He knows full well that regular giving keeps us from greed, and greed poisons everything it touches.

Of course, the biblical commands to *give* cover more than just our money; we are also to give of our time and talents, among other things.

 WE'RE STILL COMMANDED TO GIVE, BUT IT'S NO LONGER 10 PERCENT. IN ALL LIKELIHOOD, IT'S MUCH MORE!

Now, you may be asking, "Well, tithing is clearly taught in the Old Testament, but is it a New Testament doctrine as well?" Yes, under the Law, God's people were commanded to give the first 10 percent of their income, which we know as the *tithe*. (See Leviticus 27:30–34 for example.) To people still under the Law, people without the indwelling Holy

Spirit, God gives a specific requirement: you must give 10 percent of your income. (The Old Testament is prone to give very specific requirements.) But does this 10 percent requirement apply to believers in the New Testament era, after the day of Pentecost, to saints now filled with the Holy Spirit? Well, yes...and no. We're still commanded to give, but it's no longer 10 percent. In all likelihood, it's much more! (If this has caused you deep distress, and you are experiencing the innate feeling of your wallet closing even tighter, I apologize. Please take a moment to compose yourself before reading on.)

A look at several New Testament Scriptures should help to clarify this.

> *Remember this: Whoever sows sparingly will also reap sparingly, and whoever sows generously will also reap generously. Each of you should give what you have decided in your heart to give, not reluctantly or under compulsion, for God loves a cheerful giver. And God is able to bless you abundantly, so that in all things at all times, having all that you need, you will abound in every good work.*
>
> (2 Corinthians 9:6–8)

Here, Paul incorporates several of the key themes of biblical giving.

First, we are no longer compelled to give exactly 10 percent of our income. That number was given to the Jewish people, who were under the Law, not filled with the Holy Spirit. Christians are encouraged to give what we've *decided in our hearts* to give. Why? Because the Spirit indwells us and will help us determine what to give. Could it be less than 10 percent? Indeed it could. But I'm of the belief that if 10 percent was the baseline for those in Israel, the Spirit will regularly inspire and enable us to give much more than that!

Notice that we shouldn't be giving "*reluctantly or under compulsion.*" This is not about giving because God demands it and the Bible requires it. Rather, it's about giving with joy and gratitude. And how is *that* possible? How might we be joyful in giving away our own money? The secret is to first realize that it's not our money at all! Everything we have—from the clothes we wear to the money in our bank accounts, the car we drive, the phone we use, the food we eat, and even the very breath in our lungs—is all a gift from God to us. So we're not giving God 10 percent of our money anyway; He owns 100 percent and we're simply returning some for use in His kingdom.

Second, Paul draws on a basic principle regularly taught in the Bible, and it comes from a truism about farming: those who sow very little will reap very little. Makes perfect sense, right? If you only plant a few carrot seeds, you cannot expect to harvest five hundred pounds of carrots. But Paul expands the traditional application of farming into the arena of the believer's giving. In so doing, it's very possible that he's following teaching that comes directly from Jesus Himself.

> *Give, and it will be given to you. A good measure, pressed down, shaken together and running over, will be poured into your lap. For with the measure you use, it will be measured to you.* (Luke 6:38)

Here, Jesus is clearly echoing the teaching of the last of the Old Testament prophets. *"A good measure, pressed down, shaken together and running over"* sounds an awful lot like *"I will open the windows of heaven for you. I will pour out a blessing so great you won't have enough room to take it in!"* (Malachi 3:10 NLT).

Elsewhere, Jesus notes that those who give up much to follow Him will not fail to receive a hundred times as much in return, plus eternal life! (See Mark 10:30.) Again, God's blessing is inherently tied to our sacrificial giving, although it's worth noting, in opposition perhaps to some modern-day prosperity preachers, that Jesus specifically does not tie the reward to financial gain. The sacrifice He mentions is a personal one, and so the reward might very well be personal as well.

As with the principle Paul highlights in his second letter to the Corinthians, Jesus indicates that we may give whatever amount we determine to give. But Jesus quotes a Jewish proverb and thereby includes an all-important caveat: the measure you use will be measured back to you. This merits careful consideration. It sounds very much like God's generosity toward us is measured, at least in part, by our generosity toward God and other people. Now, just based on our understanding of grace and mercy—a gift God gives us that we don't deserve and exoneration from a punishment that we *do* deserve—we know that the correlation is not direct. Undoubtedly, God is more generous to us, and more consistently so, than we are to Him and others. However, the principle still applies: the measure you use is the measure that will be used to determine your blessing.

 BECAUSE SO MANY HAVE BEEN GRIPPED BY A SPIRIT OF GREED, THEY WANT TO BLESS OTHERS WITH THEIR TEASPOON, ALL THE WHILE HOPING THAT GOD BLESSES THEM WITH HIS BUCKET!

What are we to make of this? Well, Jesus is teaching that a generous spirit is welcomed by God and certainly leads to His abundant blessing on our lives. Many of us, however, seem to miss this correlation: counting on God's grace and goodness to us, we somehow feel like it's permissible to be stingy toward the work of the kingdom and toward those who walk with us in life. To use an analogy, because so many have been gripped by a spirit of greed, they want to bless others with their teaspoon, all the while hoping that God blesses them with His bucket! "Oh, here's my pocket change, Lord, but by all means, please send a few hundred dollars my way!" Jesus is teaching us a variant of the Golden Rule: as we give, so shall it be given to us. This biblical teaching on giving is very good news! As we are generous with our time and financial resources, volunteering our efforts for the kingdom of God, He promised to pour out blessings on us, and lavishly so, spilling out into every area of our lives.

THE NEGATIVE ABSOLUTES

SEXUAL IMMORALITY

Despite waning standards relative to sexual morality in both culture and the church, the Bible is quite adamant that believers are to maintain the highest ethics. Over and again, *sexual immorality* is listed as something to be avoided by God's people. To be sure, sexual morality was still a developing concept in the Old Testament; although God forbade certain deviant practices for the Jews, things such as polygamy were still widely practiced. By the time the New Testament writers are inspired, however, the call was consistent. One man and one woman for one lifetime is God's intention for human sexual expression. Over and again, we read that believers are to avoid sexual immorality. Let's look at some examples.

In his first letter to the Corinthians, Paul is dealing with people who think themselves so spiritual, so *otherworldly* almost, that they believe what's done in the body doesn't really count. They've bought into the philosophy of *Gnosticism*, which in part teaches that only *spirit* is real and true; flesh is inherently sinful and may be discounted. These Corinthians were so spiritual, in fact, that some were having sex with prostitutes because, after all, what's done in the body doesn't matter— their spirits remained pure and holy. "Nonsense!" Paul replies.

Our bodies are intrinsically valuable and holy to God; as believers, we are united with Christ, who was bodily resurrected from the dead. What's done in the flesh really does matter. Paul concludes:

> **Flee from sexual immorality.** *All other sins a person commits are outside the body, but whoever sins sexually, sins against their own body. Do you not know that your bodies are temples of the Holy Spirit, who is in you, whom you have received from God? You are not your own; you were bought at a price. Therefore honor God with your bodies.* (1 Corinthians 6:18–20)

The apostle could not be stronger: *"Flee from sexual immorality."* Avoid all forms of sex that occur outside the bonds of marriage. Our bodies were purchased at a price and are now the temples of the Holy Spirit. Paul pushes back quite hard against the Gnostic idea of dualism, stressing that both our bodies and our spirits are the Lord's and must be used for His glory. Sexual immorality is forbidden, regardless of the circumstance.

The writer to the Hebrews agrees. *"Marriage should be honored by all, and the marriage bed kept pure, for God will judge the adulterer and all the sexually immoral"* (Hebrews 13:4). In other words, marriage should be viewed as something of great value, to be highly prized, and must be treated as such.

Two extremes should be avoided. Contrary to the prevailing understanding in Greco-Roman culture, the unknown writer—who may have been one of Paul's associates—teaches that it is entirely reasonable to think that a man can uphold the sanctity of his marriage and refrain from taking mistresses on the side. On the other side, many in that culture viewed asceticism—refraining from sexual intercourse entirely—as the goal of true holiness, even within marriage. Paul combats this idea directly in 1 Corinthians 7:1–6. The New Testament teaches that a sexual relationship within the bounds of marriage is a gift from God. Those who commit adultery and practice other forms of sexual expression outside of marriage will be judged for those misdeeds.

There are numerous verses in the New Testament that list vices that believers are to avoid; in each case, sexual immorality is included. Consider Paul's instruction to the churches of Ephesus and Galatia:

> But among you there must not be **even a hint of sexual immorality**, or of any kind of impurity, or of greed, because these are improper for God's holy people. Nor should there be obscenity, foolish talk or coarse joking, which are out of place, but rather thanksgiving. For of this you can be sure: No immoral, impure or greedy person—such a person is an idolater—has any inheritance in the kingdom of Christ and of God. (Ephesians 5:3–5)

*The acts of the flesh are obvious: **sexual immorality**, impurity and debauchery; idolatry and witchcraft; hatred, discord, jealousy, fits of rage, selfish ambition, dissensions, factions and envy; drunkenness, **orgies**, and the like. I warn you, as I did before, that those who live like this will not inherit the kingdom of God.* (Galatians 5:19–21)

When Paul writes to the church at Thessalonica, he simply could not be clearer: sexual immorality is absolutely forbidden.

*It is God's will that you should be sanctified: that you should **avoid sexual immorality**; that each of you should learn to control your own body in a way that is holy and honorable, not in passionate lust like the pagans, who do not know God; and that in this matter no one should wrong or take advantage of a brother or sister. The Lord will punish all those who commit such sins, as we told you and warned you before. For God did not call us to be impure, but to live a holy life. Therefore, anyone who rejects this instruction does not reject a human being but God, the very God who gives you his Holy Spirit.*

(1 Thessalonians 4:3–8)

The apostle does not seem to be enamoured with the idea that sexual purity is an old-fashioned idea, and believers are instead free to express themselves in any manner they wish!

THINGS PAUL NEVER SAID

Oh? The culture has redefined sexuality in terms of whatever makes you feel good, or makes you happy? The old norms of keeping sex within marriage are out of vogue? Social media portrays a very different sexual ethic than the biblical view? Well, then, by all means, enjoy sexual expression in any way you see fit!

No, the command to sexual purity is an absolute, the rejection of which will be punished by God because it is rebellion not simply against those who teach it, but against the Holy Spirit Himself. The stakes could not be much higher.

 TIME AND AGAIN, SEXUAL IMMORALITY IS NOTED AMONG THE LISTS OF PRACTICES FOR WHICH GOD IS BRINGING JUDGMENT.

Finally, what really drove this point home to me was a study of Revelation in preparation for a course I was teaching. Here we have God's final thoughts on a wide variety of issues, from the perseverance of believers to the judgment of the wicked. Time and again, I noticed, sexual immorality is noted among the lists of practices for which God is bringing judgment.

> *The rest of mankind who were not killed by these plagues still did not repent of the work of their hands; they did not stop worshiping demons, and idols of gold, silver, bronze, stone and wood—idols that cannot see or hear or walk. Nor did they repent of their murders, their magic arts, **their sexual immorality** or their thefts.*
> (Revelation 9:20–21)

> *He said to me: "It is done. I am the Alpha and the Omega, the Beginning and the End. To the thirsty I will give water without cost from the spring of the water of life. Those who are victorious will inherit all this, and I will be their God and they will be my children. But the cowardly, the unbelieving, the vile, the murderers, **the sexually immoral**, those who practice magic arts, the idolaters and all liars—they will be consigned to the fiery lake of burning sulfur. This is the second death."*
> (Revelation 21:6–8)

> *Blessed are those who wash their robes, that they may have the right to the tree of life and may go through the gates into the city. Outside are the dogs, those who practice magic arts,* **the sexually immoral,** *the murderers, the idolaters and everyone who loves and practices falsehood.*   (Revelation 22:14–15)

At the very end of time, when God is describing the things for which He has sought but failed to find repentance, and for which He is therefore judging the world, sexual immorality is listed repeatedly. In the face of those who would insist that biblical sexual morals are simply limited to the first century and no longer apply to us *enlightened* souls today, Revelation reminds us that both now and at the very end—perhaps in the near future—God still considers sexual immorality to be wrong, and rewards those who remain sexually pure.

PRIDE

Although this absolute is widely known, it seems to get very little press in the church today compared to the more sensational "sins" of having female preachers, for example, or voting for the wrong political party! But pride is a sin that goes directly to the core of the human condition; it's as old as humanity itself. It's been said that all sin stems from pride, for we willingly choose our own direction, and our own desires, over those God has ordained for us. Pride says that we know better than God and are therefore in charge of our own destinies. It's an intrinsic sin, in the sense that we can faithfully follow Christ and name Him as Lord, yet struggle daily with our will versus His. In some sense, pride exists deep within all of us.

The Bible unmistakably and regularly warns us of pride, in both the Old Testament and the New. Before we look at a few examples, it's worth noting that many biblical scholars believe the very first sin in the universe—the rebellion of Satan—was actually motivated by pride. In a passage that many believe is referring to Satan's fall, Isaiah writes:

How you have fallen from heaven, morning star, son of the dawn! You have been cast down to the earth, you who once laid low the nations! You said in your heart, "I will ascend to the heavens; I will raise my throne above the stars of God; I will sit enthroned on the mount of assembly, on the utmost heights of Mount Zaphon. I will ascend above the tops of the clouds; I will make myself like the Most High." But you are brought down to the realm of the dead, to the depths of the pit. (Isaiah 14:12–15)

In these verses, we see the pride of Satan manifested: "**I will** *ascend to the heavens;* **I will** *raise my throne…***I will** *sit enthroned…***I will** *ascend above the tops of the clouds;* **I will** *make myself like the Most High."*

God is having none of it: you say you will ascend, but you are, in fact, brought down to the depths of hell itself.

The Proverbs repeatedly warn us of the dangers of pride, even telling us that God *hates* pride:

To fear the LORD *is to hate evil; I hate pride and arrogance, evil behavior and perverse speech.* (Proverbs 8:13)

When pride comes, then comes disgrace, but with humility comes wisdom. (Proverbs 11:2)

Pride goes before destruction, a haughty spirit before a fall. Better to be lowly in spirit along with the oppressed than to share plunder with the proud. (Proverbs 16:18–19)

Haughty eyes and a proud heart—the unplowed field of the wicked—produce sin. (Proverbs 21:4)

Other biblical writers echo the same idea: pride is a sin before God. John writes:

> *For everything in the world—the lust of the flesh, the lust of the eyes, and the pride of life—comes not from the Father but from the world.* (1 John 2:16)

When teaching on the evil that so easily resides in the human heart, Jesus notes that pride or arrogance is, in fact, one of the things that defiles us:

> *[Jesus] went on: "What comes out of a person is what defiles them. For it is from within, out of a person's heart, that evil thoughts come—sexual immorality, theft, murder, adultery, greed, malice, deceit, lewdness, envy, slander, arrogance and folly. All these evils come from inside and defile a person."* (Mark 7:20–23)

In perhaps the most devastating critique of the sin of pride, James quotes Proverbs 3:34 and notes clearly God's stance toward pride:

> *You adulterous people, don't you know that friendship with the world means enmity against God? Therefore, anyone who chooses to be a friend of the world becomes an enemy of God. Or do you think Scripture says without reason that he jealously longs for the spirit he has caused to dwell in us? But he gives us more grace. That is why Scripture says: "God opposes the proud but shows favor to the humble." Submit yourselves, then, to God. Resist the devil, and he will flee from you.* (James 4:4–7)

Now, I don't know about you, but life is quite hard enough without God opposing me! We all pray for God to be in our corner, and because of the grace of God, that prayer is answered. While God doesn't often remove the obstacles we face, He daily gives us grace to face each day with hope, joy, and optimism. But God opposes those who are proud. I simply cannot imagine how difficult life must be with God standing in opposition! It's likely that you too count on God's favor each day.

The sin of pride has had devastating effects on humanity and continues to pervade the human condition. We can easily see the effects of this sin throughout culture, via the millions who declare, "Not Your will, but my will!" in the face of God's commands and desires. We see the effects of pride that come from the material possessions, positions of power, and status afforded our celebrities. But looking *in the mirror* rather than *out the window,* we also see the destructive effects of pride in our own lives, and the work of the Holy Spirit to eradicate this sin from our hearts and minds. Thanks be to God for His grace and mercy, and for the Spirit who works in us to put to death sins such as pride, which so easily entangle us!

 THE SIN OF PRIDE HAS HAD DEVASTATING EFFECTS ON HUMANITY AND CONTINUES TO PERVADE THE HUMAN CONDITION.

THE BLACK AND WHITE

The preceding examples serve to remind us that although there are in fact many gray areas the believer must navigate today, there are nonetheless absolutes by which we must abide. Everything is not gray, nor is everything black and white. The Bible contains both.

We've seen that there are some things God commands us to do, including being generous with our giving and offering forgiveness. To these, we could add showing compassion (Ephesians 4:32; 1 Peter 4:8), submission (Ephesians 5:21; Hebrews 13:17), good deeds (James 2:14–17; 1 Peter 2:12), and loving our enemies (Matthew 5:44; Romans 12:14).

In addition to sexual immorality and pride, the Bible also forbids idolatry (Leviticus 19:4; 1 Corinthians 10:14), lying (Proverbs 12:22; Colossians 3:9–10), revenge (Romans 12:19; 1 Peter 3:9), and gossip or slander (Exodus 23:1; James 4:11).

In each case, God commands that we live in a particular way, doing the things He proscribes and abstaining from things that war against our soul. There is no debate about these things. Idolatry is not simply a cultural prohibition from the ancient Near East or first century, even though the form of idolatry may change with context and era. All believers are to avoid idolatry, period. Likewise, forgiveness is not optional; all followers of Christ are to forgive as the Spirit enables.

Make no mistake: these absolutes can only be followed by the power of the Holy Spirit. We are not able to remain sexually pure by self-discipline alone (remember that Jesus equated lust with adultery!), just as we're not able to avoid idolatry, offer forgiveness to someone who has hurt us deeply, or give generously when the spirit of greed is all around us. Thankfully, though God has given us absolutes by which to live, He's also given us the indwelling Holy Spirit to help us live holy lives. In chapter three, we'll explore the biblical teaching surrounding the Spirit of holiness and the Spirit's role in our lives.

SHADES OF GRAY ABOUND

But first, let's take a moment to recognize that in light of the absolutes we've mentioned, there are still quite a number of gray areas. Believers in the twenty-first century are faced daily with decisions for which there is no clear answer like, *"Flee from sexual immorality"* (1 Corinthians 6:18).

What are we to make of the heated debate in many Christian circles today about the consumption of alcohol? Why do so many believers declare that the Bible teaches tattoos are a sin, and why do so many believers insist on getting tattoos nonetheless? How should we navigate the rapidly exploding world online, including social media? How can an ancient book like the Bible speak into concerns that didn't even exist twenty-five years ago? It is to these questions and others that we now turn.

2

TINDER, TATTOOS, AND TEQUILA

Unlike the absolutes we covered in the last chapter, there are many choices faced by believers that do not come with a directive or clear command from Scripture. This may be because the Bible discusses these in a culturally restrictive manner, or perhaps because the issue at hand is particular to the twenty-first century. The world didn't have smart phones or the Internet when the Bible was written. Now, this is not to say that the Bible leaves us without instruction; it certainly does, but not in terms of an obvious command relative to the particular choice.

Let's focus now on the three examples we're using as the title of this book: *Tinder, Tattoos, and Tequila.* Each of these allows us to explore additional areas of concern for modern-day holiness. Through our discussion of alcohol, we'll explore the traditional tendency of believers (going right back to the Pharisees!) to *build fences around the Law*. The topic of tattoos allows us to examine how Christians today may use and abuse the Old Testament, particularly in terms of the Law given to Israel. Finally, few topics are more ubiquitous and commonplace than social media. Everywhere we look, the online world and the culture of social media pervade our conversation, lifestyle, and morality. How is a believer living by the precepts of a book almost two thousand years old supposed to navigate Facebook, Twitter, TikTok, and Instagram? How should we who are called to influence the world for Christ respond to the "influencers" of today, both inside the church and in the larger culture? To paraphrase the Bard, that is indeed the question!

EXAMPLE #1: TINDER

Our first example gets us into a discussion on the whole range of social media and entertainment driven by technology. I chose Tinder for the alliteration, of course, but also as representative of the many forms of social media we have access to today, from Facebook, Instagram, TikTok, and YouTube to what seems like thousands of other options in the online universe. How should Christians approach their social media usage? Can Christians play video games? If so, are any off-limits? What do we make of the rise of social media influencers, including Christian influencers within the church?

Of the three examples, this one is most easily and clearly identified as *a gray area*, if for no other reason than the Bible never mentions Twitter, Pinterest, or *Call of Duty* by name!

THINGS PETER NEVER SAID

When thou art on social media, avoid diligently those apps pertaining to sexual relationships, one with the other, ensuring also that thy games of the screen reflect righteousness and peace, not striking down in the thousands these avatars of thy fellow citizens. See to it also that thou dost not engage strangers in futile arguments; lo, those debates fought in 140 strokes of the quill or less, are poison to thy soul and the souls of those that partake in such works of iniquity.

This then is the perfect spot to stop and recognize that there are indeed gray areas in the Christian life, precisely because the Bible, as an ancient document, could not possibly address directly every one of the decisions and challenges we face in the twenty-first century. Some believers insist that life with Christ is quite black and white; I've never believed this to be true—and am less inclined to do so today. There are a myriad of decisions we must make about our values, purchases, entertainment, politics, and viewpoints that Scripture simply does not directly address.

You may be asking, "Didn't the Holy Spirit inspire the writers of old? Didn't He guide them as they put quill to parchment? If God is omniscient, would He not have known that in our era, social media would explode onto the scene, and every believer would have to make decisions about their participation, which platforms they would use, and how to conduct themselves online?"

Yes, indeed, the church has long believed that God knows the future, beginning to end, and would therefore be well aware during Paul's writing to the Romans that we'd face these challenges some two thousand years later.

In our understanding of inspiration, however, we'd do well to remember a couple of things.

DIVINELY INSPIRED WITH HUMAN AUTHORS

First, while the Bible is divinely inspired, it had very human authors. Have you ever stopped to consider how that partnership worked? I mean, we believe that God inspired Scripture in a different manner than when we say Shakespeare was inspired when he wrote *Romeo and Juliet*, or Michelangelo was inspired while painting the Sistine Chapel. The Bible itself tells us, *"All Scripture is God-breathed and is useful for teaching, rebuking, correcting and training in righteousness"* (2 Timothy 3:16). Have you ever given any thought to exactly how this God-breathed inspiration occurred? Most people haven't. Some I've met seem to think that the

Holy Spirit was so involved that He moved Luke's pen for him, dictating every word. Others view inspiration as little more than motivation, or creative help, much along the lines of inspired sculptures or frescos.

 THE HOLY SPIRIT ENSURED THAT EVERYTHING HE WANTED TO BE WRITTEN WAS RECORDED WITHOUT ERADICATING THE HUMAN PERSONALITY OF THE BIBLICAL AUTHORS.

My sense is that the Holy Spirit, working through the biblical authors, ensured that everything He wanted to be written was indeed recorded in their prophecies, history, Gospels, and letters, *without in any way eradicating the human personality of the authors*. In other words, while God's thoughts are fully included in Paul's letters, we still see plenty of Paul in the pages of Corinthians, Galatians, and Timothy. For example, in Galatians, Paul is *really* frustrated with a group of people who attached portions of the Old Testament law to a believer's newfound faith in Christ. Some older Bible translations use the term "Judaizers" for these people.

Law and grace don't mix, Paul repeatedly declares. He gets so irritated talking about those who insist, for example, that believers must be circumcised as Jews were ordered to do under the old covenant, that he rants:

> I just wish that those troublemakers who want to mutilate you by circumcision would mutilate themselves.   (Galatians 5:12 NLT)

I don't know how much of the Holy Spirit is in that verse (perhaps He's frustrated too!) but we certainly see a whole lot of Paul. If cutting off the foreskin is so powerful to save, Paul declares, then by all means, cut the whole thing off and be completely saved! (And my male readers just cringed.)

When Paul is writing to the church at Corinth, we see a moment of human frailty. He's upset that the church has become so divided, some claiming to follow Paul, others Peter, and others Apollo. He asks, "Were you baptized into the name of Paul? Aren't we all baptized in Jesus' name?" He observes:

> *I thank God that I did not baptize any of you except Crispus and Gaius, so no one can say that you were baptized in my name. (Yes, I also baptized the household of Stephanas; beyond that, I don't remember if I baptized anyone else.) For Christ did not send me to baptize, but to preach the gospel.* (1 Corinthians 1:14–17)

Even while writing under the inspiration of the Holy Spirit, Paul is having trouble remembering who he's baptized. "I only baptized two of you; no, wait—also the household of Stephanas. There may be more, but that's not really my point, people!" His struggle to remember is not a real surprise to any of us who are getting older.

Another very human moment for Paul comes in one of his last letters before his death. In 2 Timothy, Paul is bound by chains, facing more prison time alone through the winter, and is by now an elderly man for his times. He pours his heart into his letter to Timothy, giving all of the pastoral advice he's accumulated over years of faithful service. But he ends with this most revealing request:

> *When you come, bring the cloak that I left with Carpus at Troas, and my scrolls, especially the parchments.* (2 Timothy 4:13)

Paul needs a warmer cloak for the winter, and he's asking Timothy to bring it. He also needs his *books*, particularly his parchments. Paul is lonely at this point and is very much looking forward to a visit from his young protégé. But further, he has real concerns about keeping warm through the winter and is perhaps anxious to continue his study of the Scriptures, necessitating the request for his scrolls and parchments.

A very human Paul, while writing under the inspiration of the Spirit, relates some very human requests.

WRITTEN FOR SPECIFIC NEEDS

Second, while the Holy Spirit and the human authors worked in partnership to produce the Scriptures, we note that each book was written to address specific historical contexts, people, or congregations. In other words, the authors of Scripture were very much people of their times, writing in response to situations and events occurring in their lifetime.

Luke, for example, wrote his account of Jesus' life and teaching for a person named Theophilus. (See Luke 1:1–4). Although we know almost nothing about him, it seems Luke was concerned that the *"most excellent Theophilus"* (verse 3) was given a thorough account of Jesus' life.

Likewise, John writes to *"the lady chosen by God and to her children"* (2 John 1:1) and *"my dear friend Gaius"* (3 John 1:1)—real people, with real situations. First Corinthians is not only addressed to an actual church in Corinth in the first century, but it also mentions both a report that's been brought to Paul *"from Chloe's household"* (1:11) and a letter that the congregation had written to him (7:1). Paul systematically works through the issues he's heard about and those that were raised in the church's own letter. Again, a real congregation, experiencing actual historical issues that needed to be addressed.

Even the prophetic books, while predicting some things that had not yet occurred, nonetheless were written in response to particular historical situations, such as Israel's unfaithfulness (Hosea) or encouragement for first century believers living under persecution (Revelation). These also include prophetic visions to reassure the listeners that God does, in fact, have human history well under His sovereign grasp.

So, we may not divorce these books of Scripture from their original contexts. Further, we cannot expect Peter, even while writing under the inspiration of the Spirit, to alert his audience to the dangers of social media. Just imagine their confusion!

Where does this leave us then?

Just because the Bible doesn't address modern apps and entertainment directly doesn't mean it's left us without wisdom to guide our decision-making. Rather, there are a whole host of principles given in the Scriptures that may help us in these choices. As the authors of Scripture were navigating the very real issues about which they were writing, to actual historical persons and congregations, they included—through the inspiration of the Holy Spirit—a great number of godly principles and wisdom by which we are to live our lives. Just because Twitter, Facebook, and other forms of social media are not mentioned by name does not mean the Bible has left us without guidance on whether or how to participate. Video games certainly weren't envisioned when John wrote his epistles, but the principles he shared are incredibly useful today.

We have not been left alone when it comes to making these difficult decisions. God Himself dwells within us, working in us to perfect holiness.

EXAMPLE #2: TATTOOS

"Don't you know it's a sin to get a tattoo? The Bible says so!" This line has been repeated, I daresay, the world over. Scriptural "truths" like this are no respecter of persons! I cannot count the number of times a young adult has come to me—either tattooed or about to be—and given anecdotal evidence of this very thing said to them by concerned family members or spiritual leaders. To be sure, the Bible does indeed warn against tattoos:

> *Do not cut your bodies for the dead **or put tattoo marks on yourselves**. I am the* LORD. (Leviticus 19:28)

There it is in plain text. No tattoos. Yet, I'm convinced that this is another of our gray areas because of the type (or genre) of Scripture from which this verse comes and the intended application for us today.

Leviticus, as you may know, is a part of the Old Testament that contains the Law given to Israel. What you may not know is that there are three different types of Law given. Although scholars name these variously, we'll follow the Westminster Confession of Faith and go with ceremonial, civil, and moral law.

You're no doubt aware that the church today does not follow all of the laws given in the Old Testament equally. We do not, for example, send women out of town during their monthly cycle (see Leviticus 15:19) or stone our rebellious teens to death (see Deuteronomy 21:18–21). We seem to instinctively realize these laws are not to be followed by believers today. But without a clear understanding of the various types of law found in the Old Testament, we may be left with a situation where the determination of which laws are still to be followed is left up to whoever is preaching the sermon. Thus, our situation with tattoos. Let's unpack briefly these different types of Old Testament law.

CEREMONIAL LAW

These laws or statutes are called *hukkim* or *chuqqah* in Hebrew, which literally means "custom of the nation." As a rule, they apply to the nation of Israel in the Old Testament and may be regarded as focused on how God's chosen people worship, practice their faith, and walk in relationship with one another. They involve a variety of sacrifices and other modes of worship that allow the Israelites to remain in good standing before God. A number of festivals and celebrations are included that helped Israel remember that God had chosen the Jews as His people and recall the miracles He had performed in their midst. The ceremonial law includes very specific regulations governing Israel, helping to ensure that Israelites remained distinct from the idolatry that was so rampant among their neighbors. Finally, there are a number of highly symbolic requirements and events throughout the ceremonial law, such as circumcision and the Passover, that point the Jewish people to the coming Messiah.[3]

The ceremonial law no longer applies to us as believers, but it is tremendously useful for demonstrating to us just how holy God is and how abhorrent sin is. All of the required sacrifices were fulfilled in Jesus' life and death. As Hebrews teaches us, Jesus made the perfect sacrifice, once and forever, for us and our sins. We have no need to go back to the sacrificial system of the Old Testament.

JUDICIAL/CIVIL LAW

The civil laws of the Old Testament were set up so the nation of Israel would not just survive, but also thrive among its neighbors—and often its enemies. They apply to Israel as God's chosen nation-state. Many of these laws pertain to very human experiences and practices, such as dealing with blood, dead animals, and human excrement. Mishandling such things can lead to poor health and outbreaks of disease. (Scientists weren't really aware of things like bacteria until a few centuries ago.) Many of these laws were put in place for the protection of Israel, specifically in terms of their health and communal relationships. These laws no longer apply to us today because contrary to some common misconceptions, God no longer has a favored nation-state on earth. Physical Israel has become spiritual Israel; believers are citizens of God's kingdom, here on earth. Again, Jesus has fulfilled the law pertaining to Israel as God's chosen people.

---

3. "What is the difference between the ceremonial law, the moral law, and the judicial law in the Old Testament?", Got Questions Ministries, www.gotquestions.org/ceremonial-law. html. This is a simple but useful explanation on the three types of Old Testament law.

MORAL LAW

Finally, unlike the ceremonial law that was fulfilled in Jesus' life and death for our sins, and the civil law given to national Israel, the Old Testament contains moral laws that have not changed. Although they too were given to a historically situated Israel, they teach us about what God has determined is right or wrong, good or evil, righteous or unrighteous. These laws reflect the character of God which, as we know, doesn't change. All of the moral law in the Old Testament is repeated and affirmed in the New Testament.

 JESUS NOT ONLY KEPT THE MORAL LAW HIMSELF, BUT HE RAISED THE STAKES, UPPED THE ANTE, AND REAFFIRMED THE COMMANDMENT.

Jesus not only kept the moral law Himself, but whenever it was mentioned to Him, He raised the stakes, upped the ante, and reaffirmed the commandment. For instance:

> *You have heard that it was said, "You shall not commit adultery." But I tell you that anyone who looks at a woman lustfully has already committed adultery with her in his heart.* (Matthew 5:27–28)

Now, as others have noted, Jesus actually fulfilled the moral law as well, in the sense that we certainly are no longer *earning* our way to God through our good works. But rather, as we'll note elsewhere, God's Spirit living in us causes us to desire holiness and yearn to live in obedience to God's commands. We live by the moral law not because we're seeking to earn a relationship with God, but precisely because we already have a relationship with God! God's moral law reflects His righteous character, so in our efforts to become more like Jesus, we with gratitude allow the Spirit to empower us to live out the moral law of God.

So, back to tattoos. Christians often do not do a good job of distinguishing between the different types of law—and the larger culture around us does even worse! How many times have you observed a Christian quote the prohibition against homosexuality in Leviticus 18:22 and had someone slam them back with comments about eating shellfish, touching a football (a dead pig's skin), or having their rebellious teenagers murdered? (The third episode from the second season of *The West Wing* demonstrated this perfectly. You can find it on YouTube by searching "West Wing + Homosexuality.")

This scenario is happening daily in the online discussion surrounding homosexuality, and also, it so happens, when it comes to believers getting tattoos. In a very well-known example, a letter was apparently written to radio and television personality Dr. Laura Schlessinger, responding to comments she made about homosexuality that she had taken from Leviticus. I'll reproduce it here as it gives a powerful example of what I'm talking about:

> Dear Dr. Laura:
>
> Thank you for doing so much to educate people regarding God's Law. I have learned a great deal from your show, and try to share that knowledge with as many people as I can. When someone tries to defend the homosexual lifestyle, for example, I simply remind them that Leviticus 18:22 clearly states it to be an abomination...End of debate.
>
> I do need some advice from you, however, regarding some other elements of God's Laws and how to follow them.
>
> 1. Leviticus 25:44 states that I may possess slaves, both male and female, provided they are purchased from neighboring nations. A friend of mine claims that this applies to Mexicans, but not Canadians. Can you clarify? Why can't I own Canadians?

2. I would like to sell my daughter into slavery, as sanctioned in Exodus 21:7. In this day and age, what do you think would be a fair price for her?

3. I know that I am allowed no contact with a woman while she is in her period of Menstrual uncleanliness – Lev.15: 19-24. The problem is how do I tell? I have tried asking, but most women take offense.

4. When I burn a bull on the altar as a sacrifice, I know it creates a pleasing odor for the Lord – Lev.1:9. The problem is my neighbors. They claim the odor is not pleasing to them. Should I smite them?

5. I have a neighbor who insists on working on the Sabbath. Exodus 35:2 clearly states he should be put to death. Am I morally obligated to kill him myself, or should I ask the police to do it?

6. A friend of mine feels that even though eating shellfish is an abomination, Lev. 11:10, it is a lesser abomination than homosexuality. I don't agree. Can you settle this? Are there "degrees" of abomination?

7. Lev. 21:20 states that I may not approach the altar of God if I have a defect in my sight. I have to admit that I wear reading glasses. Does my vision have to be 20/20, or is there some wiggle-room here?

8. Most of my male friends get their hair trimmed, including the hair around their temples, even though this is expressly forbidden by Lev. 19:27. How should they die?

9. I know from Lev. 11:6-8 that touching the skin of a dead pig makes me unclean, but may I still play football if I wear gloves?

10. My uncle has a farm. He violates Lev.19:19 by planting two different crops in the same field, as does his wife by wearing garments made of two different kinds of thread (cotton/

polyester blend). He also tends to curse and blaspheme a lot. Is it really necessary that we go to all the trouble of getting the whole town together to stone them? Lev.24:10-16. Couldn't we just burn them to death at a private family affair, like we do with people who sleep with their in-laws? (Lev. 20:14)

I know you have studied these things extensively and thus enjoy considerable expertise in such matters, so I'm confident you can help.

Thank you again for reminding us that God's word is eternal and unchanging.

Your adoring fan,
Anonymous

(It would be a damn shame if we couldn't own a Canadian.)[4]

As a Canadian, this is of particular interest to me personally! And, I must be honest, people who bring up the laws handed down to the Jewish people in Exodus and Leviticus have a point. We cannot just keep picking single verses out of the Old Testament to enforce doctrine without recognizing that there are three specific types of law given and only the moral law, repeated in the New Testament, is applicable today.

THE OLD TESTAMENT ITSELF DOES NOT DECLARE WHETHER A GIVEN LAW IS CEREMONIAL, CIVIL, OR MORAL—AND FOR THE CHURCH TODAY, THAT DISTINCTION IS IMPORTANT.

One of the challenges is that the Old Testament itself does not declare whether a given law is ceremonial, civil, or moral. For the Jewish people, it didn't much matter because all were to be carefully followed;

---

4. James Martin, S.J., "Dr. Laura and Leviticus," *America: The Jesuit Review*, August 18, 2010 (www.americamagazine.org/faith/2010/08/18/dr-laura-and-leviticus).

breaking one was as bad as breaking another. But for the church today, that distinction is important. Now, we cannot expect the world at large to get this point, but we can certainly strive to ensure the church understands it! When it comes to the topic of tattoos, therefore, we are into a passage of instruction that is clearly within the ceremonial/civil category of law. Let's expand beyond the prohibition against tattoos in Leviticus 19:28 and examine some of the other verses in that chapter.

> When you sacrifice a fellowship offering to the LORD, sacrifice it in such a way that it will be accepted on your behalf. It shall be eaten on the day you sacrifice it or on the next day; anything left over until the third day must be burned up. If any of it is eaten on the third day, it is impure and will not be accepted. Whoever eats it will be held responsible because they have desecrated what is holy to the LORD; they must be cut off from their people. (Leviticus 19:5–8)

> When you reap the harvest of your land, do not reap to the very edges of your field or gather the gleanings of your harvest. Do not go over your vineyard a second time or pick up the grapes that have fallen. Leave them for the poor and the foreigner. I am the LORD your God. (Leviticus 19:9–10)

> Do not steal. Do not lie. Do not deceive one another. (Leviticus 19:11)

In this section, we find all three types of law. Verses 5–8 are clearly ceremonial law; they offer precise instructions on how to offer a sacrifice for sins. Verses 9–10 give civil law; God shows the Israelites very practically what it means to care for the poor. Lastly, in verse 11, we observe God's moral law: the command to tell the truth reflects exactly God's own glory, in whom is never any deception. Jesus said He was the very embodiment of truth (see John 14:6), and the Holy Spirit is called "the Spirit of truth" (John 16:13).

As part of the moral law, the command against lying is regularly repeated in the New Testament, including Colossians 3:9, where Paul plainly commands, *"Do not lie to each other."*

But what of the command about tattoos in particular? Let's look at that section of verses:

> *Keep my decrees. Do not mate different kinds of animals. Do not plant your field with two kinds of seed. Do not wear clothing woven of two kinds of material.* (Leviticus 19:19)

> *Do not eat any meat with the blood still in it. Do not practice divination or seek omens. Do not cut the hair at the sides of your head or clip off the edges of your beard. Do not cut your bodies for the dead* **or put tattoo marks on yourselves.** *I am the* LORD. (Leviticus 19: 26–28)

This whole section is designed to distinguish Israel from her cultic neighbors. Although we're not totally familiar with the pagan rituals behind some of these commands, it's apparent to biblical scholars that these instructions are designed to combat idolatry, thus placing them in the ceremonial category.

Of course, this places the decision to get a tattoo firmly in *a gray area*. Although the Bible does address it specifically, it does so in the midst of Old Testament law intended to separate Israel from its neighbors. Believers who wish to insist that tattoos are a sin because "the Bible says so!" had better ensure their vegetable gardens don't contain both carrots and potatoes, their clothes aren't polyester-cotton, and the edges of their beards are growing ever longer! Further, they must find this command repeated in the New Testament—and, happily for those of you who are tattoo fans, it isn't.

EXAMPLE #3: TEQUILA

No matter which country singer is crooning about it, the very word "tequila" is enough to send shivers down the spine of some saints. A substantial portion of the Christian world are teetotalers, to use the older word, totally abstaining from the consumption of alcohol. For some denominations, this is not a theoretical exercise or simply a matter of preference. In many cases, one cannot be a member of a local congregation, serve in leadership, or pastor a church if their lifestyle includes drinking alcohol. If they observe the Lord's Supper, the local church or assembly serves grape juice, and great efforts are expended to teach the dangers of alcohol. (I remember, as a boy, reading a book that called alcohol "the devil's juice" and warned us to stay far away from it.)

How did a group of people who follow a Man known for turning water into wine end up with such an aversion to alcohol? The Gospel of John records Jesus' first miracle, and no matter what profound theological insights you take from the story, there are a couple of key facts:

1. Jesus made between 120 and 180 *gallons* of wine, based on the size of the stone jars the Jews used for ceremonial washing. (See John 2:6.)

2. It was *really good wine*—the very best. In fact, the man in charge of the banquet told the bridegroom, *"Everyone brings out the choice wine first and then the cheaper wine after the guests have had too much to drink; but you have saved the best till now"* (verse 10).

Wine was widely used in the ancient Near East as it enabled people to safely consume fluids in an era prior to refrigeration, when clean water wasn't always available. (Centuries later, Thomas Bramwell Welch, a Methodist, perfected his recipe for pasteurizing grape juice because he was firmly opposed to using real wine in Communion.)

Surely, given the extreme stance some groups take on the issue, there must be clear biblical teaching on the avoidance of alcohol. Undoubtedly, this must be one of the absolutes?

THINGS JESUS NEVER SAID

Thou shalt not ever, under any circumstances, consume fermented fruit of the vine, under pains of an eternity in hellfire and brimstone!

Obviously, if Jesus is at a wedding feast and turning water into wine, He doesn't oppose alcohol. In fact, the Bible does mention alcohol multiple times, but only in terms of abuse. The consumption of alcohol is one of those topics where the Bible gives us both an absolute and notes a gray area. Let's first look briefly at the absolute: the prohibition against drunkenness. The clearest command is probably the one given by Paul when writing to the church at Ephesus:

> *Do not get drunk on wine, which leads to debauchery. Instead, be filled with the Spirit.* (Ephesians 5:18)

It's hard to get much blunter than that. The challenge with drunkenness—or intoxication of any kind, for that matter—is that we lose control of ourselves and rarely make the best decisions. Intoxication impairs our judgment, the truth of which so many have become painfully aware.

THE CHALLENGE WITH DRUNKENNESS—OR INTOXICATION OF ANY KIND—IS THAT WE LOSE CONTROL OF OURSELVES AND RARELY MAKE THE BEST DECISIONS.

Instead, Paul teaches, we should give control of ourselves over to the Holy Spirit, who will always lead us into good decisions—actions that reflect the character of Christ. Voluntary loss of control via intoxication is unbecoming for the follower of Christ, who is regularly encouraged to remain sober, watchful, and careful in both speech and action. Throughout the New Testament, drunkenness is included in the vice lists we discussed earlier. For example:

> *The acts of the flesh are obvious: sexual immorality, impurity and debauchery; idolatry and witchcraft; hatred, discord, jealousy, fits of*

rage, selfish ambition, dissensions, factions and envy; **drunkenness,**
*orgies, and the like. I warn you, as I did before, that those who live
like this will not inherit the kingdom of God.* (Galatians 5:19–21)

*Or do you not know that wrongdoers will not inherit the kingdom of
God? Do not be deceived: Neither the sexually immoral nor idola-
ters nor adulterers nor men who have sex with men nor thieves nor
the greedy nor* **drunkards** *nor slanderers nor swindlers will inherit
the kingdom of God.* (1 Corinthians 6:9–10)

Let us behave decently, as in the daytime, not in carousing and
drunkenness, *not in sexual immorality and debauchery, not in dissension and jealousy.* (Romans 13:13)

Clearly, drunkenness falls outside of God's best for our lives. It
belongs to those who do not know Christ, those who do not yet walk in
the light of the truth of the gospel. So there's our absolute. Why then
do so many Christians also make an issue of alcohol consumption per
se? Obviously one glass of wine, or a beer enjoyed during a meal with
friends, will not cause intoxication. The answer in part lies in our tendency to "build a fence around the law." This concept likely comes from
Deuteronomy 22:8: *"When you build a new house, make a parapet around
your roof so that you may not bring the guilt of bloodshed on your house if
someone falls from the roof."* In other words, take precautions to ensure
that not only do you not transgress the law, but you've built a fence to
make sure you don't get anywhere close to doing so.

And so, in the time of the Old Testament, there sprung up a great
many laws, "traditions of the elders," that were designed to keep Jews from
breaking one of God's actual commands. For example, Deuteronomy
25:3 states that a guilty person who is being flogged as a punishment for
his crime may receive no more than forty lashes. Rabbis subsequently
ruled, therefore, that thirty-nine was the highest number allowed, to

ensure that the law would not be broken by accident or miscounting. Now, these leaders undoubtedly had good motives; they were seeking to avoid the transgression of the Law. In reality, however, by Jesus' time, these *fences* had become a law unto themselves, and breaking one was considered just as serious as breaking the actual commands of God.

We see this in Matthew 15, in which Jesus and His disciples are chastised for not properly cleansing their hands before eating. They broke *"the tradition of the elders"* (verse 2). Jesus is having none of that. He asks, *"Why do you break the command of God for the sake of your tradition?"* (verse 3). In a statement that should give all of us serious pause for thought, He tells them, *"You nullify the word of God for the sake of your tradition"* (verse 6). That is, the *fence* now has a greater priority than the thing it was designed to protect!

In many ways, those who teach total abstinence from alcohol have built a fence around drunkenness. If you don't take the first drink, of course, it is impossible to get drunk. I should pause here and note that there are many good reasons for a believer to choose to refrain from alcohol. In parts of the world, such as where I currently live, alcoholism is a serious cultural issue. Many Christians are dedicated to ministering to those caught in this deadly addiction and so avoid alcohol altogether. In some cases, though, the community has been taught over the years that Christians abstain, so the believer who drinks socially on occasion may damage their own witness. Yet this is a case of the community confusing the fence with the command. Despite these good and biblical motives, it simply cannot be argued that the Bible prohibits the consumption of any alcohol whatsoever. It only warns against drunkenness and abuse. Consider this oft-cited example:

Who has woe? Who has sorrow? Who has strife? Who has complaints? Who has needless bruises? Who has bloodshot eyes? Those who linger over wine, who go to sample bowls of mixed wine. Do not gaze at wine when it is red, when it sparkles in the cup, when it goes down smoothly! In the end it bites like a snake and poisons like a viper. Your eyes will see strange sights, and your mind will imagine confusing things. You will be like one sleeping on the high seas, lying on top of the rigging. "They hit me," you will say, "but I'm not hurt! They beat me, but I don't feel it! When will I wake up so I can find another drink?"   (Proverbs 23:29–35)

This Scripture clearly has the abuse of alcohol in mind; it's hard to imagine this scenario coming to pass after a single drink with dinner. Unlike abuse and drunkenness, consumption really is *a gray area*. The fact remains, therefore, that believers may, in good conscience, consume alcohol responsibly. But should we?

In our next two chapters, we will explore how the indwelling Holy Spirit can help us navigate the gray areas of faith, and the way the Bible uses principles of godly living to assist us with modern choices.

3

THERE'S NO "HOLY" WITHOUT THE HOLY SPIRIT

We're now entering the meat of this discussion, as it were, and the core of what we're hoping to accomplish. The next five chapters will unpack the questions that *we must ask the Holy Spirit* when navigating the gray areas of life and practice:

1. Is this right (or wrong) for me to do?

2. What are the principles of the Word that guide my participation?

3. By doing this, might I cause someone who is weaker in the faith than I am to copy me and thus do something that is sinful for them?

4. By doing this, might I damage my reputation and witness to Jesus in the larger community outside of the church?

5. Is this wise?

The answers to each of these questions will contain a basic biblical principle and an example or two so we can flesh out exactly what we're talking about. First, we must consider the role of the Holy Spirit in this process, for He's deeply involved in the entire thing!

THE HOLY WHO?

Together with the Father and the Son, the Holy Spirit makes up the Godhead, the Three-in-One. Now, admittedly, wrapping our heads around the Spirit is not an easy task. As New Testament scholar Gordon D. Fee related, "A student once told a colleague of mine: 'God the Father makes perfectly good sense to me; and God the Son I can quite understand; but the Holy Spirit is a gray, oblong, blur!'"[5]

Many of us can relate to this student. We can envision and identify with the Father and the Son in some ways, but the Holy Spirit? That's another matter! As believers, we hear so much these days about *living life in the Spirit, walking with the Spirit,* and so forth. So often, unfortunately, we are eager to walk with Someone we don't really know much about.

Without getting lost in the weeds, we'll begin by noting that the Holy Spirit is one third of the Trinity, our triune God. While the word "trinity" is not found in the Bible, the concept surely is. The church has long believed that although God is One, the Bible teaches that the Godhead is composed of the three persons: Father, Son, and Holy Spirit. A few Scriptures should suffice to make this clear. In his second letter to Corinth, Paul declares:

---

5. Gordon D. Fee, *Paul, the Spirit, and the People of God* (Peabody, MA: Hendrickson Publishers, 1996), 24.

*May the grace of the **Lord Jesus Christ**, and the love of **God**, and the fellowship of the **Holy Spirit** be with you all.*

(2 Corinthians 13:14)

Matthew's baptismal formula, quoted as the words of Jesus Himself, reflects the same:

*Then Jesus came to them and said, "All authority in heaven and on earth has been given to me. Therefore go and make disciples of all nations, baptizing them **in the name of the Father and of the Son and of the Holy Spirit**, and teaching them to obey everything I have commanded you. And surely I am with you always, to the very end of the age."* (Matthew 28:18–20)

Finally, for me, one of the most powerful examples of the Trinity in Scripture is found in the story of Jesus' baptism:

*Then Jesus came from Galilee to the Jordan to be baptized by John. But John tried to deter him, saying, "I need to be baptized by you, and do you come to me?" Jesus replied, "Let it be so now; it is proper for us to do this to fulfill all righteousness." Then John consented. As soon as **Jesus** was baptized, he went up out of the water. At that moment heaven was opened, and he saw the **Spirit of God** descending like a dove and alighting on him. And **a voice from heaven** said, "This is my Son, whom I love; with him I am well pleased."*

(Matthew 3:13–17)

In what must be one of the coolest portions of Scripture ever, we get to see the entire Trinity at once, in the same scene! The Son is in the water, the Spirit descends on Him in the form of a dove, and the Father declares His pleasure from heaven. What a baptismal service! Even revival services don't get any better than this!

THE PERSONHOOD OF THE SPIRIT

Another important concept to consider when discussing the Holy Spirit is what it means to believe that, as with the Father and the Son, the Spirit is also a *person*.[6] I think it's fairly easy to believe and understand the Father and the Son; after all, the very names given to them in the Bible correspond easily to people we can envision in our own lives. But the Spirit is often described in less personal terms.

In Acts 2, for example, He comes from heaven with *"a sound like the blowing of a violent wind"* (verse 2) and appears as *"tongues of fire"* (verse 3). Paul described the Spirit as a *"seal of ownership"* or a *"deposit"* guaranteeing our inheritance in Christ. (See 2 Corinthians 1:22.) Of course, the biblical name predominantly given, Spirit, is much less easily associated with personhood than Father or Son. But yet, we believe the Holy Spirit is indeed a divine person.

You may not have thought much about what it means to be a person. It's one of those concepts we tend to take for granted. But when it comes to the Godhead, it's helpful for us to consider the question, "In what sense are the members of the Trinity *persons?*"

At the very least, scholars tell us that a basic definition of personhood is *self-awareness*. That is, a person is aware that he or she exists. It sounds a bit strange, perhaps, but as Descartes reminded us, "I think, therefore I am." The Father, for example, says *"I"* and *"my"* at Jesus' baptism. (See Matthew 3:17.) Asked at His trial whether He is the Messiah, the Son emphatically tells the high priest, *"I am"* (Mark 14:62). The Father and Son are clearly self-aware.

A passage that many of us have undoubtedly read, but likely not in terms of defining the Spirit's personhood, is the fascinating account in Acts 13:

---

6. For a helpful reference on this subject, see: Graham A. Cole, *He Who Gives Life: The Doctrine of the Holy Spirit* (Wheaton, IL: Crossway Books, 2007), 65–69.

*Now in the church at Antioch there were prophets and teachers: Barnabas, Simeon called Niger, Lucius of Cyrene, Manaen (who had been brought up with Herod the tetrarch) and Saul. While they were worshiping the Lord and fasting, the Holy Spirit said, "Set apart for **me** Barnabas and Saul for the work to which **I** have called them." So after they had fasted and prayed, they placed their hands on them and sent them off.*   (Acts 13:1–3)

Did you catch that? The Holy Spirit says, *"Set apart for me…for the work to which I have called them."* The Spirit is clearly self-aware. He also calls people by name for specific tasks! So much interesting information contained in so few verses.

THE HOLY SPIRIT IS CLEARLY SELF-AWARE, AND HE CALLS PEOPLE BY NAME FOR SPECIFIC TASKS.

In John 14:16, Jesus describes the Spirit as *"another advocate"* (some Bible translations say comforter, encourager, or counselor), continuing the personal activities of Jesus Himself. The Spirit will teach the disciples and bear witness to Christ (verse 26), and will convict the world, guide the disciples into truth, hear and speak, glorify and declare. (See John 16:8–15.) These are clearly activities associated with the work of a person. Further, though the Greek word for Spirit, *pneuma*, is neuter (neither masculine nor feminine), John uses the masculine pronoun continually:

*And I will ask the Father, and he will give you another advocate to help you and be with you forever—the Spirit of truth. The world cannot accept **him**, because it neither sees **him** nor knows **him**. But you know **him**, for **he** lives with you and will be in you.*
                            (John 14:16–17)

*But when **he**, the Spirit of truth, comes, **he** will guide you into all truth. **He** will not speak on **his** own; **he** will speak only what **he** hears, and **he** will tell you what is yet to come.* (John 16:13)

Now, the point of this is not to argue that the Holy Spirit is male, for although male and female genders are God's gift to us, the Godhead encompasses both. However, God cannot be thought of strictly in terms of human gender at all. Rather, the point here is that John, quoting Jesus, gives a very personal face to the ethereal Spirit of God.

In Romans 8, Paul writes of the leading of the Spirit (verse 14), witness of the Spirit (verse 16), and help of the Spirit (verse 26).

*For all who are **led by the Spirit of God** are children of God. So you have not received a spirit that makes you fearful slaves. Instead, you received God's Spirit when he adopted you as his own children. Now we call him, "Abba, Father." For his Spirit joins with our spirit to affirm that we are God's children.* (Romans 8:14–16 NLT)

*And the Holy Spirit helps us in our weakness. For example, we don't know what God wants us to pray for. But the Holy Spirit **prays for us** with groanings that cannot be expressed in words.*
(Romans 8:26 NLT)

*And the Father who knows all hearts knows what the Spirit is saying, for the Spirit **pleads for us** believers in harmony with God's own will.* (Romans 8:27 NLT)

Paul also describes the most personal of activities—the prayer of the Spirit and the Spirit's heart. If the Spirit were simply divine energy, that description would be very confusing. The Holy Spirit is obviously more than "power" or some impersonal force at work in the world.

Further, according to Paul, the Spirit may be grieved:

*And **do not grieve the Holy Spirit** of God, with whom you were sealed for the day of redemption.* (Ephesians 4:30)

I think we can all agree that while power may be resisted, only a person may be grieved. The New Testament also suggests that the Spirit displays emotions such as love and jealousy:

*I urge you, brothers and sisters, by our Lord Jesus Christ and by **the love of the Spirit**, to join me in my struggle by praying to God for me.* (Romans 15:30)

*Do you think Scripture says without reason that **he jealously longs** for the spirit he has caused to dwell in us?* (James 4:5)

Finally, in a passage that should be well-known to those familiar with the gifts of the Spirit, we read:

*Now to each one the manifestation of the Spirit is given for the common good. To one there is given through the Spirit a message of wisdom, to another a message of knowledge by means of the same Spirit, to another faith by the same Spirit, to another gifts of healing by that one Spirit, to another miraculous powers, to another prophecy, to another distinguishing between spirits, to another speaking in different kinds of tongues, and to still another the interpretation of tongues. All these are the work of one and the same Spirit, and he distributes them **to each one, just as he determines**.* (1 Corinthians 12:7–11)

Reading with an eye to the personhood of the Spirit, we must ask, "Would an impersonal force possess a will?" Clearly, when it comes to His gifts, the Spirit distributes them as He wills—yet another testament to the Spirit's personhood.

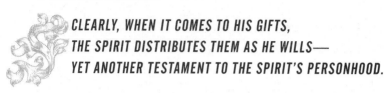

CLEARLY, WHEN IT COMES TO HIS GIFTS,
THE SPIRIT DISTRIBUTES THEM AS HE WILLS—
YET ANOTHER TESTAMENT TO THE SPIRIT'S PERSONHOOD.

I took you on this detour to consider the Spirit as a divine person because the Holy Spirit *is* a person, and we may enjoy a personal relationship with Him, just as we do with Christ. We may talk to the Spirit, seek His counsel, get to know His mind and His will, and enjoy the Spirit's guidance in our lives. In describing this, there's a particular story in the New Testament I'd now like to explore, for few others better capture what we're seeking as we journey throughout this book.

KNOWING THE MIND OF THE SPIRIT

I have long been fascinated by a verse in Acts 15 that describes an amazing knowledge of the Holy Spirit. The very young church was trying to figure out how much of their Judaism should be carried forward into the practice of their faith in Jesus.

> *Certain people came down from Judea to Antioch and were teaching the believers: "Unless you are circumcised, according to the custom taught by Moses, you cannot be saved." This brought Paul and Barnabas into sharp dispute and debate with them. So Paul and Barnabas were appointed, along with some other believers, to go up to Jerusalem to see the apostles and elders about this question.*
>
> (Acts 15:1–2)

The apostles all met together in Jerusalem to consider the matter; we know it today as the council at Jerusalem. Peter spoke quite passionately. The assembly listened to Paul and Barnabas report the miracles they had seen God perform among the gentiles. James declared that, yes indeed, God's will was to also see the gentiles come to know Jesus. Keep in mind that for a group of Jewish believers, raised on the idea that only *they* were God's chosen people, this was revolutionary teaching! Finally, they struck a balance between offending young Jewish believers and living free of the Law by the truth of God's grace. But the really startling part is how they expressed themselves, in a letter they wrote to convey their decision:

> **It seemed good to the Holy Spirit and to us** *not to burden you with anything beyond the following requirements: You are to abstain from food sacrificed to idols, from blood, from the meat of strangled animals and from sexual immorality. You will do well to avoid these things.* (Acts 15:28–29)

Did you catch that? "*It seemed good to the Holy Spirit and to us.*" Wow! Figuring out how to live holy lives by grace isn't always easy; it's the subject of this whole book. The apostles had come together, listened to each other, and discussed the matter. But at the end of the day, they were able to say with confidence: this plan seems good to us, and also to the Holy Spirit. They knew His mind in the matter! And that, friends, is the goal of living holy lives by grace: we get to know the mind of the Spirit, seeking His guidance and hearing His voice, as we make our decisions.

THE SPIRIT AND HOLINESS

Now, having determined the Spirit's place in the Trinity, and understanding that His personhood opens up for us the possibility of a relationship, let's look at how the Bible portrays the Spirit's role in our holiness. We'll start with a couple of Old Testament passages that foreshadow or prophesy God's intention before concluding with some New Testament teaching.

The first is found in Numbers 11. "Pastor" Moses is having some serious challenges with his very large congregation. (The children of Israel numbered in the millions.) His people were grumbling, as people do, and Moses has just about had enough. He complains bitterly to the

Lord, who instructs him to bring seventy of Israel's elders to the tent of meeting. The Lord explains:

> *I will take some of the* **power of the Spirit** *that is on you and put it on them. They will share the burden of the people with you so that you will not have to carry it alone.* (Numbers 11:17)

This they do, and the elders all cooperate...except for two. "Brothers" Eldad and Medad simply refuse to attend the revival service! Yet, for reasons known only to God, they too prophesy as the Spirit rests upon them. Young Joshua, feeling perhaps a touch protective over Moses' reputation, immediately informs his mentor and asks whether he should put a stop to their insolence. Moses' reply is very instructive for us:

> *Are you jealous for my sake? I wish that all the LORD's people were prophets and that the LORD would put his Spirit on them!* (Numbers 11:29)

Moses instinctively understands that God's gift of the Spirit is something that can only be helpful to both believers and leaders in the long run. He understands Joshua's concern, but doesn't agree.

The prophet Ezekiel gives us perhaps the clearest picture in the Old Testament of God's plan for the future holiness of His people. Speaking to the Israelites about days yet unseen—and prophetically describing the day of Pentecost recorded in Acts 2—Ezekiel quotes God as declaring:

> *I will give you a new heart and put a new spirit within you; I will remove from you your heart of stone and give you a heart of flesh. And I will put my Spirit in you and move you to follow my decrees and be careful to keep my laws.* (Ezekiel 36:26–27)

The external code can never bring about the kind of righteousness that God requires; a heart transplant is needed. God will replace our fossilized, insensitive heart—a biblical symbol of our emotion and will—with a soft heart of flesh that's better able to respond to His loving direction. Further, not only is God going to *give* us a new heart, He's going to put His Holy Spirit *in* us. The indwelling Spirit will cause us to follow God's statutes; we are no longer left on our own, trying to do right as best as we're able, struggling daily with our sin nature.

It's worth noting here that generally, in the Old Testament, the Holy Spirit was not the possession of believers; He instead *came upon* chosen individuals for God-ordained tasks and would typically withdraw once the task was completed. This surely was a radical message for Ezekiel's audience, accustomed as they were to the Spirit simply empowering folks for service. It shows just how important it is for the Holy Spirit to be involved in our pursuit of holiness.

 IN THE OLD TESTAMENT, THE HOLY SPIRIT CAME UPON CHOSEN INDIVIDUALS FOR GOD-ORDAINED TASKS AND WOULD TYPICALLY WITHDRAW ONCE THE TASK WAS COMPLETED.

Moving into the New Testament, let's highlight four passages that provide insight: John 14–16, Acts 2, Romans 8, and Galatians 5.

The Gospel of John contains some of the best teaching to be found on the Spirit's role in the believer's life. Jesus is comforting His disciples in preparation for His death and eventual ascension. He tells them that He's going to send *"another advocate"* to be with them when He's gone. (See John 14:16.) That word *"another"* there is important. We sometimes have trouble imagining just what kind of advocate the Spirit is; we may be encouraged, however, by Jesus' description of the Spirit as another advocate, helper, or counselor—just like Jesus. What you've seen Jesus do, the Spirit will do. The Spirit, He teaches, will be known by the disciples, for *"he lives with you and **will be in you**"* (verse 17)—clearly foreshadowing the day of Pentecost that is soon to come.

Focusing on our particular concern in this chapter, the Holy Spirit will be instrumental in helping the disciples live a holy life by grace. Jesus said:

> *But the Advocate, the Holy Spirit, whom the Father will send in my name, will **teach you all things** and **will remind you** of everything I have said to you.* (John 14:26)

That's a great assurance, right there! Though Jesus is no longer physically with us, He's not left us without help. Rather, the indwelling Spirit will be our teacher, guiding us in our decisions, and reminding us of Jesus' own teaching. Later, Jesus elaborates further:

> *But when he, the Spirit of truth, comes, **he will guide you into all the truth**. He will not speak on his own; he will speak only what he hears, and he will tell you what is yet to come. He will glorify me because it is from me that he will receive what he will make known to you. All that belongs to the Father is mine. That is why I said the Spirit will receive from me what **he will make known to you**.* (John 16:13–15)

In this passage, we learn one of the Spirit's key roles in our lives: He guides us into all truth. Certainly, when we're discussing issues such as consuming alcohol, using social media, or figuring out a Christian response to the politics of our day, having this divine person guide us into truth is a welcome benefit! Who can't use direct access to the truth when working through such issues?

ONE SPIRIT...AND MANY OPINIONS

As an aside, why is it that Christians so strongly disagree on some of these areas? If we all have the same Holy Spirit, why isn't there more unity and more agreement? Why are some Christians convinced of one stance, and others the polar opposite? Why do some say we must belong to one political party, but others passionately differ?

The short answer is that while the Spirit's guidance is perfect, our human hearing and understanding are not. Our own humanity, our preconceptions, our upbringing, and our intentionality or lack thereof all contribute to our comprehension of the Spirit's guidance. God certainly could have created a system by which He directly downloaded relevant information to us! But instead, He allows us each to work out our own salvation, with fear and trembling, knowing that on some things we will differ—and strongly so.

Prior to His ascension, Jesus told His disciples to wait for the promised baptism of the Holy Spirit, saying, "*You will receive power when the Holy Spirit comes on you; and you will be my witnesses...to the ends of the earth*" (Acts 1:8). The disciples did as they were instructed, and sure enough, the Holy Spirit fell upon those gathered on the day of Pentecost:

> *When the day of Pentecost came, they were all together in one place. Suddenly a sound like the blowing of a violent wind came from heaven and filled the whole house where they were sitting. They saw what seemed to be tongues of fire that separated and came to rest on each of them. All of them were filled with the Holy Spirit and began to speak in other tongues as the Spirit enabled them.* (Acts 2:1–4)

On that day, as one worship song notes, "The church of Christ was born, then the Spirit lit the flame."[7] Moses' desire, Ezekiel's prophecy, and Jesus' proclamation were all fulfilled at once. The Holy Spirit has now come to indwell the church!

Paul emphasizes this fact a number of times.

> *Don't you know that you yourselves are God's temple and that God's Spirit dwells in your midst?* (1 Corinthians 3:16)

> *Do you not know that your bodies are temples of the Holy Spirit, who is in you, whom you have received from God? You are not your own.* (1 Corinthians 6:19)

And what a difference that makes!

In his letter to the Romans, Paul really brings these themes into focus. After spending seven chapters outlining the challenges associated with living under the Law apart from the Spirit, Paul begins chapter 8 by declaring that none of us are under condemnation any longer, for the

---

7. Hillsong Worship, "King of Kings," on *Friends in High Places* (Hillsong, 1995).

Spirit of life has set us free from the law of sin and death. He further declares:

> Those who live according to the flesh have their minds set on what the flesh desires; but those who live in accordance with the Spirit have their minds set on what the Spirit desires. The mind governed by the flesh is death, but the mind governed by the Spirit is life and peace.
>
> (Romans 8:5–6)

OUR MINDS DECIDE WHETHER TO ENGAGE IN THAT GOSSIP, RESPOND HARSHLY ON SOCIAL MEDIA, OR CLICK THAT LINK WE KNOW WE SHOULD AVOID.

A couple of things jump out at us from these verses. First, our minds are tremendously important in all of this. If you stop and think about it, it's always the mind that makes the decision either toward righteousness, or its own, often selfish, desires. Our minds decide whether to engage in that gossip, respond harshly on social media, or click that link we know we should avoid. Yes, we all struggle with fulfilling the desires of what the Bible calls *our flesh* rather than following the Spirit's lead. Paul himself described his own battle in Romans 7.

> I do not understand what I do. For what I want to do I do not do, but what I hate I do. And if I do what I do not want to do, I agree that the law is good. As it is, it is no longer I myself who do it, but it is sin living in me. For I know that good itself does not dwell in me, that is, in my sinful nature. For I have the desire to do what is good, but I cannot carry it out. For I do not do the good I want to do, but the evil I do not want to do—this I keep on doing. Now if I do what I do not want to do, it is no longer I who do it, but it is sin living in me that does it. So I find this law at work: Although I want to do

good, evil is right there with me. For in my inner being I delight in God's law; but I see another law at work in me, waging war against **the law of my mind** *and making me a prisoner of the law of sin at work within me. What a wretched man I am! Who will rescue me from this body that is subject to death? Thanks be to God, who delivers me through Jesus Christ our Lord! So then, I myself* **in my mind** *am a slave to God's law, but in my sinful nature a slave to the law of sin.* (Romans 7:15–25)

The Bible teaches us that even though we are indwelt by the Holy Spirit, we still must contend with our old sinful nature. Paul observes that his mind is set on doing what the Spirit desires, but every day, he must contend with the sin that remains in his old self! The struggle is real. He doesn't always do the things he knows he should, and those things he's determined to avoid…well, those are the things he does. It's so encouraging to know that the apostle of old struggled with the same kinds of things we do today!

The key really is a transformed mind, a mind renewed by the Spirit. Later in this epistle, Paul writes, *"Do not conform to the pattern of this world, but be transformed by* **the renewing of your mind***"* (Romans 12:2). This transformation doesn't happen by changing your wardrobe or cutting your hair, as dictated by some of the fundamentalist types, nor exchanging one set of political or social views for another, as mandated by our *woke* friends. Rather, it's a renewed mind—a mind made new by a relationship with the person of the Holy Spirit.

Concluding that thought in chapter 8, Paul teaches that it's by the Spirit that we're able to *"put to death"* our natural inclination to sin. He writes:

Therefore, brothers and sisters, we have an obligation—but it is not to the flesh, to live according to it. For if you live according to the flesh, you will die; but if by the Spirit you put to death the misdeeds of the body, you will live. (Romans 8:12–13)

The Spirit's role in navigating the gray areas really comes to the fore when Paul discusses the fruit of the Spirit. At first, the connection might not be obvious, so allow me to unpack it. In Galatians 5, Paul is again teaching how living holy lives by grace, with the Spirit's help, is different than trying to follow God's law through our own efforts. We've been set free, he proclaims, and we are now able to live in freedom—so don't allow yourself to be bound up anymore! The primary imperative, or command, of the whole passage is found in verse 16. Verse 17 picks up his earlier theme from Romans 7:

> So I say, **walk by the Spirit**, and you will not gratify the desires of the flesh. For the flesh desires what is contrary to the Spirit, and the Spirit what is contrary to the flesh. They are in conflict with each other, so that you are not to do whatever you want.
>
> (Galatians 5:16–17)

There's the command: walk by the Spirit. That's our goal every day as we live our lives for God, seeking to please Him in word, thought, and action. Paul then moves into a vice list, as we discussed earlier in this book, before juxtaposing that with a life led by the Spirit:

> The acts of the flesh are obvious: sexual immorality, impurity and debauchery; idolatry and witchcraft; hatred, discord, jealousy, fits of rage, selfish ambition, dissensions, factions and envy; drunkenness, orgies, and the like. I warn you, as I did before, that those who live like this will not inherit the kingdom of God. But **the fruit of the Spirit** is love, joy, peace, forbearance, kindness, goodness, faithfulness, gentleness and self-control.　　(Galatians 5:19–23)

This fruit encompasses the character of God Himself, growing in us supernaturally, as the Spirit leads and guides our lives. Although many Christians today are more focused on the *gifts* of the Spirit, such as healing, prophecy, or speaking in tongues, we should recognize that the *fruit* is every bit as important as the gifts—perhaps even more so. Although I believe the gifts are given by the Spirit to any believer who is available and willing to serve, the fruit comes through continued faithfulness in our walk with God. Therefore, the true measure of *spirituality* in the New Testament is never the gifts; it's always the fruit.

THE FRUIT OF THE HOLY SPIRIT COMES THROUGH CONTINUED FAITHFULNESS IN OUR WALK WITH GOD.

Paul ends this section with one of those verses that I personally consider my *life verse*. It's only a few words, but it really packs a punch:

Since we live by the Spirit, let us keep in step with the Spirit.

(Galatians 5:25)

Note that Paul assumes believers are living by the Spirit. I often wonder if he would write the same words today! Yet I'm reminded again of Dr. Fee's observation that in the first century, there was no confusion: *all* believers were Spirit-filled. Fee writes:

> For early believers, it was not merely a matter of getting saved, forgiven, prepared for heaven. It was above all else to receive the Spirit, to walk into the coming age with power. They scarcely would have understood our...terminology—"Spirit-filled Christian." That would be like saying "Scandinavian Swede..." For them, to be Christian meant to have the Spirit, to be a "Spirit-person." To be "spiritual," therefore, did not mean to be some kind of special Christian, a Christian elitist (except perhaps at Corinth, where that was their failure). For them, to be spiritual meant to be a Christian—not over against a nominal (or carnal, etc.) Christian, but over against a non-Christian, one who does not have the Spirit.[8]

8. Gordon D. Fee, *Gospel and Spirit: Issues in New Testament Hermeneutics* (Peabody, MA: Hendrickson Publishers, 1991), 114.

So Paul can truly say, *"**Since** we live by the Spirit"*—as in, there's no other way to live! But note also what he says next: *"Let us **keep in step** with the Spirit."* Just as in Galatians 5:1, where Paul reminds us that we are in fact *set free*, so that we're able to *live* in freedom (two different things), here we live *by* the Spirit, so that we're able to *keep in step* with the Spirit (two different things). Sadly, one can be set free, yet never live in that freedom. So too, one can live by the Spirit, but never actually keep in step with the Spirit.

At this point, we've come full circle in our discussion of the Holy Spirit and His role in our lives. Understanding the Spirit as a divine person, with whom we can have a relationship, and knowing the mystery that the Spirit makes His dwelling within us, we see that we are able to keep in step with the Spirit. This speaks not only to His leading in terms of God's plan for our lives, or the way He guides us to pray, but also applies as we daily seek to walk before God in righteousness, following God's will as the Spirit enables us. It applies as we seek to navigate the many gray areas of life that we're faced with today: decisions, practices, and opportunities for which the Bible gives no clear command, as it does with the various absolutes we note throughout Scripture.

With the indwelling Spirit, we always have a helper to whom we can turn. We're able to inquire of Him no matter what decision we're facing, whether it's our use of technology, a relationship issue, or something else entirely.

OUR FIRST QUESTION

When faced with any gray area, the first question we should ask is a very simple one:

Holy Spirit, is this right or wrong for me to do?

That's it.

We should involve the Holy Spirit in all of our decisions, no matter how *ordinary* we might view them:

+ Should I leave my current job and seek something else?

+ Am I spending my money on purchases that reflect God's best for me and the world?

+ We would like to purchase a new home; is that a good idea for us right now?

And then, of course, there's the whole raft of issues with moral overtones:

+ What apps are fine for me to use?

+ Is it a good use of my time to be on Facebook three hours a day?

+ Is my presence on social media glorifying to God, or not?

+ Is it okay for me to drink alcohol responsibly, or should I abstain altogether?

+ Holy Spirit, should I get a tattoo? You know all my friends have one, and I reeeaaalllly want one! I'll even make it a Bible verse or a Christian symbol, so we can consider it *witnessing by tattoo!*

(I'm certain that last example applied more to some of you than to people like me!)

So when faced with the gray areas of life—and all of our decisions, really—we can seek guidance from the One who indwells us, given for our help and holiness, *"the Spirit of truth"* (John 16:13) who will never lead us astray. But we cannot leave this chapter without facing a key fact: when asking the Spirit whether something is permissible for us, it is critical that we honestly listen.

HEARING WHAT WE WANT TO HEAR

As humans, we have a long history of hearing exactly what we want to hear and failing to hear what we do not want to accept. I cannot count how many young couples have sat in my office, so deeply in love, as they tell me that they are "praying hard" about their next steps. Sometimes, that's just awesome. But other times, I know from the conversation that their relationship is ill-fated and unwise. Respect is missing, or control and condescension are the norm. And *still* they tell me that they've prayed about it, but "haven't heard" God tell them they should get out. I've reminded them that when emotions are involved, passions run high, and friends or family members try to influence us, hearing from God can be a real challenge.

So too with some of the gray areas we face. Hearing the Spirit say "No!" when we really want to hear a "Yes!" is challenging, no doubt. *But it's not impossible.* With a heart set toward obedience, being intentional to hear His voice, and with friends or family seeking God with us, we can hear the Spirit clearly and be obedient.

WITH A HEART SET TOWARD OBEDIENCE, BEING INTENTIONAL TO HEAR HIS VOICE, AND WITH FRIENDS OR FAMILY SEEKING GOD WITH US, WE CAN HEAR THE SPIRIT CLEARLY AND BE OBEDIENT.

If you ask the Holy Spirit, "Is this right or wrong for me to do?" and He plainly and firmly says, "No, it is wrong," then that's all there is to it. You don't really need to ask the remaining questions at all. But other gray areas will surely arise, where you initially hear a resounding, "Yes!" For those times when the Spirit confirms that a certain thing is permissible for you to do, you now move to the second key question: "Holy Spirit, what are the principles of the Word that will guide me in this?" And for that, we'll turn to chapter four.

PRINCIPLES ARE PRINCIPAL

In chapter three, we explored the role of the Holy Spirit in helping us live holy lives by grace, including navigating through the kinds of things for which the Bible gives no direct command or direction. We asked the all-important first question, "Holy Spirit, is this right (or wrong) for me to do?"

Our next question is:

Holy Spirit, what are the principles of the Word that guide my participation?

As I observed, if the Spirit says "No" to the first question, then you're done. If you ask, "Should I play this particular video game?" and the Spirit responds with a resounding, "No!" then obedience is your next course of action.

But if the answer is "Yes," we still have some work to do. Moving on to our second question, we need to know whether the Scriptures contain principles to guide us as we engage in the action about which we've asked. While the Bible may not speak directly to our situation—it does not, for instance, give the command, "Thou shalt not play *Grand Theft Auto*"—it does indeed give principles of holy living that apply to every circumstance in which we could ever find ourselves. The ideas we're going to cover are very straightforward, but absolutely necessary as we engage the gray areas of life and faith.

OLD VS. NEW TESTAMENT APPROACH

I think the first thing we should observe is that the Old Testament tends to focus more on absolutes, while the New Testament hones in on principles. Now, it's not all of one, or all of the other, in any case. Both the Old and the New Testaments give absolutes *and* principles. But the priority for the Old Testament seems to fall along the lines of giving absolute commands. It's important to recognize this and understand the reasons why this is so.

In the Old Testament, we're reading about God's chosen people, Israel, and the very tortuous story of their journey with God. Sometimes, they were faithful to His covenant; many times, they were not. When they were faithful, they enjoyed victory over their enemies; when they rebelled, they were delivered over to their enemies, in defeat, as punishment.

God gave Israel the Law—composed of ceremonial rules, judicial or civil regulations, and moral laws—three different types of laws but all of them applicable in their relationship to the God who chose them. Now, in many ways, this Law was destined to fail, and God knew that. Why? Because the people of God in the Old Testament were still dead in their sins. They had not yet received the new life available to us today through Jesus' death and resurrection. Sin had not yet been defeated.

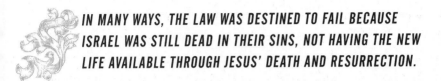

IN MANY WAYS, THE LAW WAS DESTINED TO FAIL BECAUSE ISRAEL WAS STILL DEAD IN THEIR SINS, NOT HAVING THE NEW LIFE AVAILABLE THROUGH JESUS' DEATH AND RESURRECTION.

The Law was given, Paul tells us, to teach us about sin and its deadly consequences. (See Romans 7 and Galatians 3.)

Hebrews 9 tells us that the sacrificial system was put in place by God to *cover over* the sins of Israel, looking ahead to the day when Jesus' own sacrifice would completely cleanse our consciences from all sin.

As we've observed, in Old Testament times, the Holy Spirit would simply come upon certain chosen individuals, to empower them to complete certain tasks. *"The Spirit of the Lord came upon"* Samson, Gideon, Ezekiel, or another person, and they did whatever God commanded them to do with supernatural power.

But until the day of Pentecost, the Holy Spirit did not indwell God's people. This is important to note because when you're dealing with people still dead in sin, who relied on the sacrifices of birds and animals to ensure they weren't immediately struck dead in God's presence, a whole lot of absolutes are the way to go. Make the rules concrete, make a pile of them, and make the consequences serious. The Old Testament has rules for just about everything, from what to eat and what to wear to how to make loans, when to pay workers, and more. There's even this:

> If two men are fighting and the wife of one of them comes to rescue her husband from his assailant, and she reaches out and seizes him by his private parts, **you shall cut off her hand. Show her no pity.**
>
> (Deuteronomy 25:11–12)

Unbelievable, isn't it? The Old Testament gives firm absolutes, both in how specific the law is and how awful the penalty.

There are whole swaths of the Old Testament given over to laws just that precise: absolutes, with no room for movement. (Thankfully, as we discovered earlier, only the moral laws of the Old Testament are applicable to New Testament believers!) Sadly, some who read the Bible never make the shift in their understanding from the attitude of the Old Testament to that of the New. They see God—and the Christian faith—as all about rules and regulations. It's a common refrain, and one with which I'm sure you're familiar. Many believers push back and declare that, in fact, following Jesus is not about rules, but about relationship! But it's admittedly hard to get that message across, even when we try hard daily to do so.

OLD TESTAMENT PRINCIPLE: JUSTICE

Of course, there are many examples of principles in the Old Testament, but for our purposes, we'll take a look at one of them—justice—as it helps us navigate gray areas.

> He has shown you, O mortal, what is good. And what does the Lord require of you? To **act justly** and to love mercy and to walk humbly with your God. (Micah 6:8)

Amos records God ranting, as it were, along a similar line, in a passage that we'd all do well to carefully consider today:

> I hate, I despise your religious festivals; your assemblies are a stench to me. Even though you bring me burnt offerings and grain offerings, I will not accept them. Though you bring choice fellowship offerings, I will have no regard for them. Away with the noise of your songs! I will not listen to the music of your harps. But **let justice roll on like a river**, righteousness like a never-failing stream! (Amos 5:21–24)

We see God's concern for justice in these passages. Although there is no specific command explaining how *"to act justly,"* we hear God's heart in the matter. God so desires justice that it seems He is frustrated with worship coming from those who call His name, yet allow injustice and unrighteousness to thrive.

Sometimes, admittedly, the issues we face are complex. We hear reports of police abuse and hear demands for police departments to be defunded or abolished. We hear about racial injustice and hear about demonstrations or riots, where anger flows into the streets. Where's a Christian to stand? At the very least, we recognize God's desire for justice. Each of us may land different places in terms of the very sensational and often incredibly sad stories that seem to happen all too frequently. Yet as believers in Christ, we may at least stand with resolve in our understanding that God desires justice and righteousness to flow through our congregations and communities. God is *never* in favor of injustice.

A MODERN ISSUE OF INJUSTICE

As I wrote the first draft of this chapter, news had broken in Canada and around the world that the bodies of 215 First Nations' children—whose ancestors were native to this land going back thousands of years—had been found at just a single church-run residential school in British Columbia. Just two weeks later, 751 unmarked graves were found at a single school in Saskatchewan. The Truth and Reconciliation Commission of Canada estimated that up to six thousand First Nations' children may have died at schools across the country.

For those unfamiliar with this Canadian story, from the 1880s until the last school closed in 1996, approximately 150,000 native children were removed from their parents, often forcibly by the police. They were placed in these residential schools set up by the government for the express purpose of trying to eradicate all aspects of indigenous culture. Many of these children regularly suffered physical, sexual, emotional, and psychological abuse; they were punished severely for speaking a single word in their native tongue, with thousands ultimately perishing in this abhorrent system.[9] To make matters much, much worse, the schools were run by four of the major Christian denominations in the country; all of this abuse and these deaths were perpetrated by priests, nuns, pastors, or church employees. How people who said they followed Christ could perpetrate such horrors upon innocent children boggles the mind and vexes the soul.

How might we respond to such devastating news? How do we process the feelings of an entire country enraged that children were treated so maliciously? How do we navigate the anger voiced by our fellow citizens that, of all entities, the *church* was responsible for these atrocities? Not easily, to be sure. Most of us are ashamed that so-called fellow Christians were responsible for these abuses and deaths. We wish desperately that the cause of Christ was not harmed so deeply in this country by those wearing the symbol of the cross. What should we do, and how might we respond?

Ripping children from their families and subjecting them to abuse is definitely not a gray area; it's an injustice that God abhors. Jesus says:

> *Let the little children come to me, and do not hinder them, for the kingdom of heaven belongs to such as these.*   (Matthew 19:14)

> *If you cause one of these little ones who trusts in me to fall into sin, it would be better for you to have a large millstone tied around your neck and be drowned in the depths of the sea.* (Matthew 18:6 NLT)

We know Jesus is always on the side of the children, and that's helpful. But the principles we've gleaned from the Old Testament also tell us that God is on the side of justice. In fact, God is so much on the side of justice that if we're complicit in the great injustices of our time, He'd prefer that we put our worship services on hold and work first on

---

9. News, survivor stories, reports, and additional information is available at nctr.ca.

our approach to justice and righteousness. As James clearly teaches us, *"Faith without deeds is dead"* (James 2:26). We may certainly have to listen humbly to those who have been wronged, educate ourselves, and then lend our voices and actions to the cause of justice. It's the very least we can do.

IF WE'RE COMPLICIT IN THE GREAT INJUSTICES OF OUR TIME, GOD WOULD PREFER THAT WE PUT OUR WORSHIP SERVICES ON HOLD AND WORK FIRST ON OUR APPROACH TO JUSTICE AND RIGHTEOUSNESS.

NEW TESTAMENT PRINCIPLES

SELF-CONTROL

Let's begin this section by considering an example we used earlier: alcohol consumption. As we noted, biblical teaching on this subject contains both an absolute and a principle: drunkenness is forbidden, yet alcohol may be consumed. Having covered the command against intoxication already, let's now look at how the principles in Scripture guide us in our decisions relative to fermented fruit of the vine and distilled barley, hops, and other grains. We'll do this by noting just a few of the verses that mention one fruit of the Spirit: self-control.

For the Spirit God gave us does not make us timid, but gives us power, love and self-discipline. (2 Timothy 1:7)

The end of all things is near. Therefore be alert and of sober mind so that you may pray. (1 Peter 4:7)

Make every effort to add to your faith goodness; and to goodness, knowledge; and to knowledge, self-control; and to self-control, perseverance; and to perseverance, godliness. (2 Peter 1:5–6)

For the grace of God has appeared that offers salvation to all people. It teaches us to say "No" to ungodliness and worldly passions, and to live self-controlled, upright and godly lives in this present age. (Titus 2:11–12)

Evidently, God places a high value on our ability to be self-controlled, and He lauds the importance of exercising personal discipline in our lives, increasingly so as the times grow darker and more evil is manifested. Although alcohol is not specifically highlighted in these verses, we know from the Bible's many commands against gluttony that we're to eat and drink in moderation. The principle of self-control and sobriety teaches us that while consuming alcohol will be fine for many believers—if the Holy Spirit has said "yes"—we are to do so with moderation, so that we remain fully in control of our mental and physical faculties.

Moderation, self-discipline, and self-control, will help us with a great number of other areas. Consider, for example, our use of social media or video games. It's so easy for hours to pass each day while we mindlessly thumb through others' posts or face one more quest. As God has only given us twenty-four hours in each day to enjoy life and serve His kingdom, and we sleep for six to eight of those hours (or twelve, like some teens I know!), an average of three to five hours spent daily online or watching TV may not be the best use of our time.

Further, self-control is an incredibly important principle as it governs our interactions online. It's so easy to become a *keyboard warrior* who confidently expresses opinions and harsh judgment through the Internet, saying things one would never dare to express in person. Self-control will help us to think through things we post, or responses we make, always asking whether Christ is well-represented in our online presence.

WHAT'S ON YOUR MIND?

While these principles are certainly helpful, moderation and self-control don't necessarily help us choose *which* games or social media to use. Here is another passage of Scripture that's chock-full of principles to help us with gray areas:

> *Finally, brothers and sisters, whatever is true, whatever is noble, whatever is right, whatever is pure, whatever is lovely, whatever is admirable—if anything is excellent or praiseworthy—think about such things.* (Philippians 4:8)

Here, Paul is giving advice on what we should set our minds upon. As we discovered earlier, the mind is of incredible importance in the Christian life. American radio personality and author Earl Nightingale said the strangest secret throughout history, the key to success or failure, is that we become what we think about. (I'm sitting here right now, thinking about being skinny!)

 IF WE TAKE PAUL'S SUGGESTIONS TO HEART, WE CAN GUARD OUR MINDS BY PONDERING THOSE THINGS THAT ARE TRUE, NOBLE, RIGHT, PURE, LOVELY, ADMIRABLE, EXCELLENT, AND PRAISEWORTHY.

If we take Paul's suggestions to heart, we can guard our minds by pondering those things that are:

+ True
+ Noble
+ Right
+ Pure
+ Lovely

- Admirable

- Excellent

- Praiseworthy

That's quite the list! Given Paul's teaching that *"the mind governed by the Spirit is life and peace"* (Romans 8:6), this list of things to dwell on certainly seems to fit right in with that theme. To be sure, Paul is focusing on the kinds of things we should think upon and the attributes upon which our thought life should rest. Yet I can't help but feel that we have been given excellent advice here not just for our thinking specifically, but more generally for the whole arena in which we use our minds and what we allow to invade our thoughts.

We must admit that the video games we play, the movies and TV shows we watch, the music we listen to, the social media we consume, and the material we read all have quite a substantial impact on our minds. I've heard that by age eighteen, a person has witnessed over 200,000 acts of violence and 16,000 murders, just on TV alone. Add in the content viewed via social media and video games, and those numbers are likely to be much higher. This simply has to have an impact over time.

There's little doubt that online activity, video games, and movies are all gray areas by our definition, since the Bible mentions none of those by name.

Now I should confess that within the denomination of my childhood, watching movies was very much an absolute, as in "absolutely not!" This was supported, somehow, by 1 Thessalonians 5:22 (KJV): *"Abstain from all appearance of evil."* Going to the movie theater was a sin; *do not pass Go, do not collect $200!* Then, around the time I was fifteen, as if a sign from God to my young soul, Billy Graham released an evangelistic movie. My elders were hardly sure what to make of it, so it was called a "film," pronounced okay, and that was that! We could watch Christian films!

ABSTAINING FROM THE APPEARANCE OF EVIL

As an aside, 1 Thessalonians 5:22 has long been used to control believers' behavior and turn gray areas into those that are plainly black and white. Taught by leaders who were no doubt well-meaning, this is an example of using a verse to build a rather large fence around the law. Their thinking was that some movies contain evil, therefore all movies have the *"appearance of evil."* Rock, metal, hip hop, and rap music contain many themes that we would not classify as godly, therefore all of it has the *"appearance of evil."*

The challenge in part comes from a poor translation in the King James Version (the *Holy Bible, New International Version* simply says, *"Reject every kind of evil"*) and in part from the fact that defining *"appearance of evil"* tended to be left in the hands of the leaders who were in control, not the followers of Christ seeking to live by grace.

Worse, this verse has been extrapolated to include or exclude people, with the thinking being, "Christians are better off associating only with other Christians," for example, or deciding that someone with an addiction, an unsavory lifestyle, or a habit of making poor choices has the *"appearance of evil"* and must be avoided.

This latter idea Paul explicitly rejects, as it seems the church in Corinth similarly misunderstood this principle.

I wrote to you in my letter not to associate with sexually immoral people—not at all meaning the people of this world who are immoral...But...anyone who claims to be a brother or sister but is sexually immoral. (1 Corinthians 5:9–11)

Paul's teaching here is to avoid explicit evil within the church, not to avoid entire genres of music or folks who make poor choices.

Given that our social media usage and entertainment choices are gray areas—provided that our choice has passed muster after we asked the first question, "Holy Spirit, is this right (or wrong) for me to do?"—we seek to evaluate what principles the Bible teaches that might apply. And certainly, Paul's list in Philippians 4:8 has a great deal to say to us about these choices. At the risk of repetition, but for the sake of education, imagine your favorite movies, music, reading materials, social media, or video games. Then with these in mind, look again at this list. Paul is teaching us to think on, and therefore participate in, whatever is:

+ True
+ Noble
+ Right
+ Pure
+ Lovely
+ Admirable
+ Excellent
+ Praiseworthy

Now, I'm certain we're getting the point, and wow, I'll confess, it's really difficult to filter so much of our entertainment and online choices today through this list! It is, however, such a valuable exercise. Placing our choices beside these things that Paul tells us to fill our minds with should certainly give us additional guidance when it comes to navigating the gray areas.

 PLACING OUR CHOICES BESIDE THE THINGS THAT PAUL TELLS US TO FILL OUR MINDS WITH SHOULD GIVE US ADDITIONAL GUIDANCE WHEN IT COMES TO NAVIGATING THE GRAY AREAS.

How do your movie or music choices stack up against this list? What about the video games that you may enjoy? How might our online lives be better governed if this list were kept close at hand? How might it impact the conversations we have about others? (Gossip, anyone?) Take a moment and consider your answers to those questions.

LAWFUL VS. BENEFICIAL

You may recognize this principle, which comes right from Paul's first letter to the church at Corinth. As we noted, throughout the epistle, Paul responds to a letter they've written to him. He is dealing with an issue that was highly contentious for the first-century church: food offered to idols. (We'll explore this more thoroughly in the next chapter.) Of interest here is the fact that Paul quotes their letter back to them in order to refute their point. The Corinthians, it seems, were big believers in grace—so much so that they had begun to really abuse their freedom in Christ, participating in sins such as sexual immorality (chapters 5 and 6), and failing to distinguish between the natural differences in the genders (chapter 11). Under grace, they proclaimed, we're free to do as we wish! Not so fast, the apostle responds. Addressing sexual immorality, he says:

> *"I have the right to do anything," you say—but not everything is beneficial. "I have the right to do anything"—but I will not be mastered by anything. You say, "Food for the stomach and the stomach for food, and God will destroy them both." The body, however, is not meant for sexual immorality but for the Lord, and the Lord for the body.* (1 Corinthians 6:12–13)

Later, he uses their words when explaining the freedom they have as believers:

> *"I have the right to do anything," you say—but not everything is beneficial. "I have the right to do anything"—but not everything is*

constructive. No one should seek their own good, but the good of
others. (1 Corinthians 10:23–24)

Paul gives us a principle that should really serve us well when navigating gray areas. Although under grace, believers certainly are free, and we may feel we have the *right* to engage in various behaviors or make certain choices, Paul counters with the truth that not all decisions are beneficial or constructive.

Further, we must not seek our own good all the time, but rather we should seek the good of others. In the gray areas, our decisions often impact those around us. As Christians, we are called to put others first, even when it comes to our choice of video games or music. We'll unpack this concept further in the next chapter.

A SLEIGHT OF HAND

For this New Testament principle, we'll look directly to the teaching of Jesus. In Matthew 6, Jesus is challenging the tendency of the religious leaders of His day, the Pharisees, to make public spectacles of both their gift-giving and their prayers. It seems they liked to really show off when they gave gifts and made sure that everyone within earshot could hear their passionate and pious prayers! Jesus basically says, "Nope, that's not how you're supposed to do things. Not at all."

Be careful not to practice your righteousness in front of others to be seen by them. If you do, you will have no reward from your Father in heaven. So when you give to the needy, do not announce it with trumpets, as the hypocrites do in the synagogues and on the streets, to be honored by others. Truly I tell you, they have received their reward in full. But when you give to the needy, do not let your left hand know what your right hand is doing, so that your giving may be in secret. Then your Father, who sees what is done in secret, will reward you. And when you pray, do not be like the hypocrites, for they love to pray standing in the synagogues and on the street corners

*to be seen by others. Truly I tell you, they have received their reward
in full. But when you pray, go into your room, close the door and
pray to your Father, who is unseen. Then your Father, who sees what
is done in secret, will reward you.* (Matthew 6:1–6)

Now, I don't know about you, but a quick survey of those I'm following on my own social media accounts tells me that this passage is incredibly relevant today. Although Jesus uses two very particular examples, His general principle is taught right in that first verse: "Don't practice your righteousness in front of others, in order to be seen and praised by them." God's reward and the reward we receive from others are mutually exclusive. If you want esteem, applause, and commendations from trumpeting your good works to everyone, Jesus says, go ahead. But don't expect God to follow up with His own reward.

We may decide to give to others—and we should. We may be involved in various kinds of ministry—and that's great. But should we talk about our good deeds online? That's quite another question. The bottom line is, "What is our motive?" It can be tricky to figure out our own reasons, let alone those of others! But it's imperative that we regularly check our own hearts and our motivation for doing the things we do.

**IT'S IMPERATIVE THAT WE REGULARLY CHECK OUR OWN HEARTS
AND OUR MOTIVATION FOR DOING THE THINGS WE DO.**

For example, we may post online that we've contributed to one cause or the other. Are we doing so to elicit praise from those who notice, or to encourage others within our sphere of influence to likewise give to this worthy cause? We may have been involved in some very successful, life-changing ministry, and wish to share that with as many people as possible. Again, it's wise to check our motives. Are we looking for our reward from those reading? Or seeking to give God glory for the great things *He* is doing? Only you can answer that question.

STAY IN YOUR OWN LANE

One final principle from the New Testament will also serve us well before we begin the next chapter. Consider these verses:

*You, then, why do you judge your brother or sister? Or why do you treat them with contempt? For we will all stand before God's judgment seat…So then, **each of us will give an account of ourselves to God**. Therefore let us stop passing judgment on one another. Instead, make up your mind not to put any stumbling block or obstacle in the way of a brother or sister.* (Romans 14:10–13)

*Therefore, my dear friends, as you have always obeyed—not only in my presence, but now much more in my absence—**continue to work out your salvation with fear and trembling**, for it is God who works in you to will and to act in order to fulfill his good purpose.* (Philippians 2:12–13)

This principle might be summarized as, "Keep your own life straight, and mind your business!" The Bible regularly teaches that we each will give an account of our lives to God. (Happily, I should note, it's the God of grace and mercy who'll be sitting on that throne, and not one of the many who unfairly judge us!) Further, it teaches that as you live your life by grace, stop judging others who are trying to do the same. Stay in your own lane, as it were.

A STORY ABOUT EARRINGS AND FEET…

"God said, 'If you want me to heal you, then you must take out your earrings!'"

Did God actually say that? You would think so, if you had heard a testimony in my local church when I was a teenager. A young lady was struggling with some kind of physical ailment with her feet, and was seeking God for healing. God's apparent response was, "If you want healing, remove your earrings." The young lady did as she was instructed; lo and behold, she was healed! I kid you not.

Do I believe this story was true? I do indeed; I knew well the person involved. Do I think God really cares that much about earrings? No, not at all. Is it possible earrings had become a symbol of rebellion for this young woman, raised as she was in our legalistic context? It surely is. Is it possible these earrings had drifted from a simple fashion statement into some kind of idolatry? Yes, it's quite possible. Did God perhaps use this strange request as a means of testing her faith and obedience? Yes, I think that's how He often works, as Scripture bears out.

So what's the issue then?

As I recall, the point of the testimony was to declare to the congregation that *everyone should avoid wearing earrings*. If it's wrong for one of us, surely it's wrong for all! And therein lies the problem. If you were raised in a very legalistic, or black and white church environment, the idea is clearly taught that *sin is sin*. Period. What's wrong for one is wrong for all. But the Bible doesn't bear that out, at least not in terms of the gray areas. As we'll see, Paul explicitly teaches that some things can be quite fine for some believers, but sin for others.

This doesn't apply to the absolutes, mind you. But for the various gray areas we encounter every day, we each may receive different answers to the five questions I'm outlining in this book. So on our own journey of life and faith, it's imperative that while we seek counsel from the Holy Spirit, and endeavor to live obediently to the direction He gives, we must also not judge or lambast those whose choices are different. The world is increasingly polarized and, sadly, we cannot honestly say the church is of one accord. Division exists everywhere, including within the body of Christ. While we are commanded to walk with each other, bear one another's burdens, and provide accountability to each other in terms of the absolutes, we're also taught that we're not to judge one another based on differing choices in the gray areas.

In our next chapter, we will delve more fully into the idea that something can be permissible for one believer, but sin for another. Even if something is perfectly fine for us individually, its impact on a fellow believer who is weaker in the faith may ultimately render it wrong for us as well. We'll examine closely Paul's instruction on this theme by working through the apostle's teaching on two of the first century's gray areas: eating of food offered to idols and eating meat. And we'll use his teaching to arrive at our third question—one of utmost importance that's rarely asked.

5

OH, WHEN THE SAINTS GO STUMBLIN' DOWN

I was raised in the Pentecostal tradition. Christians did not drink alcohol, period. But my first pastorate was with a wonderful group of believers from a variety of church backgrounds; the congregation itself was not affiliated with a particular denomination. Unbeknownst to me, they were in the custom of toasting their new pastors with some quality champagne. Imagine my surprise when upon confirmation of my hiring, the board of elders pulled out a bottle to celebrate! And picture their surprise when I said that we didn't drink—because we were Christians! They were confused, and we were embarrassed. They quickly found some ginger ale for me and my wife.

Another time, we had a new Iraqi friend at our home for a meal. A medical doctor, she is a faithful believer and follows one of the oldest forms of Christianity, a branch of what is now the Roman Catholic Church. When invited, naturally, she brought wine, as is their custom. Upon hearing that we don't consume alcohol, she exclaimed, "Oh! You must be Muslim!"

I could not have been more shocked. "Of course not!" I replied. "We're Pentecostals."

She thought for a moment, then said, "Oh, I see, you're *Pentecostal Muslims!*"

I almost fainted. You see, in their culture, you knew who was Muslim very quickly by their abstinence from alcohol. The Christians partook, as did the Jews; only the Muslims refused. We quickly navigated that funny misunderstanding!

Christians who come out of the world's major Christian traditions, including Roman Catholicism, the Church of England, and those who are children of the Reformation, generally see no issue with the moderate consumption of alcohol. As we noted earlier, it's drunkenness that's the absolute, after all. But other believers, who come out of the eighteenth century holiness movement—including groups like the Salvation Army, Pentecostals, Methodists, and some Baptists—have typically avoided alcohol altogether. There are a variety of reasons for this, including involvement in temperance movements and a desire to minister to those experiencing alcoholism.

 ONE UNFORTUNATE CONSEQUENCE OF "BUILDING A FENCE AROUND THE LAW" IS THAT IT KEEPS BELIEVERS IN A STATE OF IMMATURITY.

Further, these children of the holiness movement have tended to do something common to the Pharisees: in chapter two, we called it "building a fence around the law." This is the idea that if something is a sin—drunkenness, for example—then staying as far away from it as possible must be a good idea. And, in principle it is. But it tends to lead to the creation of a great many "laws" and "sins" to keep believers far from the absolute given in Scripture. One unfortunate consequence is that it keeps believers in a state of immaturity. So many things are *sin* that they don't need maturity or wisdom to make wise decisions around a particular issue; they just need to follow the rules. How do we navigate this real-world issue?

Thus far, we've considered the first two questions we must ask when trying to navigate the gray areas of faith:

- Holy Spirit, is this right (or wrong) for me to do?
- Holy Spirit, what are the principles of the Word that relate to the choice I'm facing?

If God has given you clarity on the first question and you've proceeded to determine what principles apply to your decision, you're now ready to face the next question:

Holy Spirit, by doing this, might I cause someone who is weaker in the faith than I am to copy me and thus do something that is sinful for them?

IT'S A FACT OF LIFE THAT WITHIN THE CHURCH, WE ARE AT VARYING LEVELS OF MATURITY, SPIRITUAL STRENGTH, AND CHRISTLIKENESS.

JUST WHO ARE THE WEAK?

In my experience, this question is rarely asked. Sure, we're aware that some people have served God for a very long time, and others are brand new to the faith. We might even realize that some who are new seem to mature very quickly and…(whisper) some who've been on the road a long time don't appear to have matured very much at all!

It's a fact of life within the church: we are at varying levels of maturity, spiritual strength, and Christlikeness. The Bible teaches, for example, that those of us who are strong should really help out when someone messes up, bearing their burdens for them. (See Romans 15:1.) In his first letter to the church at Corinth, Paul grumbles that he still has to feed them milk, not solid food; they're so divided and they argue so much, they're *"mere infants in Christ"* (1 Corinthians 3:1). Hebrews 5:11–14 describes exactly the same scenario in another community.

In Romans 14, Paul makes it plain that some will be mature, and others will be immature. He's not blaming the latter, as he does in 1 Corinthians 3. Instead, he's describing those who are *weak in the faith* because *they're new Christians.* They're immature because they're babies, so to speak, newly born into the kingdom of God. Because they're new to the faith, and not as mature as other brothers and sisters, they tend to struggle with some things out of their past and are not able to approach some issues with the confidence that their *elder* sisters and brothers have.

For the apostle, this includes things like eating food that's been sacrificed to idols. For twenty-first century believers, however, it might be something like consuming alcohol, even in moderation. As we've noted, in some Christian circles, this is quite the issue; in others, far less so. Given that drunkenness is the absolute, how do we navigate the gray area of *social drinking* in some of our contexts? Well, it turns out that in dealing with a particular first century situation, Paul has given some incredibly practical advice.

YOUR SISTER, HOLY DAYS, AND THE MEAT YOU EAT

In Romans 14, in a section that various Bible translations have entitled, "The Weak and the Strong," Paul describes three primary issues that were of significance in the first century: the eating of meat (verse 2); the observance of certain holy days (verse 5); and the drinking of wine (verse 21). A few verses will give you an idea of the issues:

> *Accept other believers who are weak in faith, and don't argue with them about what they think is right or wrong. For instance, one person believes it's all right to eat anything. But another believer with a sensitive conscience will eat only vegetables...In the same way, some think one day is more holy than another day, while others think every day is alike. You should each be fully convinced that whichever day you choose is acceptable.*
>
> (Romans 14:1–2, 5 NLT)

Now, scholars are still debating exactly what was going on behind the scenes for these things to be an issue. Were the *"weak"* folks gentile Christians, recently out of idolatry and pagan backgrounds, who were carrying their old dietary laws and holy day observances into their newly found place in the body of Christ? Or were they Jewish believers, still trying to fulfill the law of Moses from the Old Testament? We're not entirely sure; it seems the Romans knew what Paul was talking about so well that he didn't have to bother to explain it! In any case, we have the strong and the weak. The weak won't eat meat, they observe certain days, and they abstain from wine. The strong see nothing wrong with any of it. So Paul has two groups in his Roman church; how should they proceed? His advice here brings us to the crux of the matter, and begins our discussion on this chapter's principle: *in all things, consider the weaker brother and sister.*

"DISPUTABLE MATTERS" ARE THE GRAY AREAS OF THE CHRISTIAN LIFE, THINGS UPON WHICH BELIEVERS WILL DISAGREE.

Paul states the theme of his advice, right in the first verse: accept believers who are weaker in faith than you are, and don't argue with them about right or wrong. Another translation states, *"Accept the one whose faith is weak, without quarreling over disputable matters"* (NIV). These *"disputable matters"* are the gray areas of the Christian life, things upon which believers will disagree. They aren't the absolutes we described earlier. Rather, they are decisions upon which believers will have legitimate differences of opinion. Paul's advice, right from the start, comes across in one single verse: accept other believers who are weaker in the faith, and stop arguing about matters that are disputable.

Paul points out that all believers are servants of God, and he asks, *"Who are you to judge someone else's servant?"* (verse 4). In the very next verse, he teaches that whether the Romans choose to observe certain days or not, *"Each of them should be fully convinced in their own mind."* This is good advice. Paul is saying that no matter which side you fall on in this particular debate, you need to be fully convinced of your position. It's not enough, therefore, for the weaker brother just to follow the lead of one who is stronger. Nor is it satisfactory for the stronger one to hold a position just to be different than the one perceived to be weaker. No matter what position you hold, it should be thoroughly considered, weighed against Scripture, and held with confidence.

It's worth noting here that Paul is probably assuming that the believers will put into practice his teaching earlier in this epistle:

Those who live in accordance with the Spirit have their minds set on what the Spirit desires. The mind governed by the flesh is death, but the mind governed by the Spirit is life and peace.

(Romans 8:5–6)

In Romans 12:2, Paul admonishes that we should not be conformed any longer to the patterns of this world—including how we approach gray areas—but we should be transformed by the renewing of our minds. Then, he says, we can *"test and approve what God's will is."* This, of course, could not be more relevant to our present discussion.

Having carefully considered our position, and being fully convinced of it, Paul really comes to the heart of the matter: each of us will have to give an account to God for our actions—and none of us will be able to blame anyone else! Given that:

Let's stop condemning each other. Decide instead to live in such a way that you will not cause another believer to stumble and fall.

(Romans 14:13 NLT)

"Stop condemning each other." That's a solid piece of advice for believers throughout the ages, and it's certainly needed today. We see much condemnation in the world and must do our part to reduce it in the church. Again, Paul is echoing his earlier teaching. He begins the magnificent chapter 8 by declaring, *"There is now no condemnation to those who are in Christ Jesus."* If God Himself does not condemn believers, then surely believers can cease condemning one another.

His next counsel in Romans 14:13 is also full of wisdom: *decide to live in such a way that you will not cause another believer to stumble and fall.* What's really powerful about this is the way that Paul acknowledges the power of the free will God has given us. Our ability to choose is one of the marks, or signs, of the image of God in us from creation itself. (See Genesis 1:27.) We have free will as a gift of God. Paul tells us to use our free choice to live in such a way that is beneficial to others. That becomes the basis of his entire teaching on this topic—and ours.

I am convinced, being fully persuaded in the Lord Jesus, that nothing is unclean in itself. But if anyone regards something as unclean, then for that person it is unclean. If your brother or sister is distressed because of what you eat, you are no longer acting in love. Do not by your eating destroy someone for whom Christ died.

(Romans 14:14–15)

Here Paul teaches an important principle: when it comes to the disputable matters, the gray areas, believers can and will have differences of opinion. He is quite certain—on the authority of Jesus Himself—that no food is forbidden, that everything is given by the providence of God for our good. But for the weaker brother or sister, perhaps due to their past connection with idolatry or poor teaching, certain foods are wrong.

EVERYTHING IS GIVEN BY THE PROVIDENCE OF GOD FOR OUR GOOD, BUT FOR THE WEAKER BROTHER OR SISTER, CERTAIN THINGS MAY BE WRONG.

We further learn here that it's possible to be right...and then act wrongly. Yes, for us, the food might be just fine, but if it causes distress for the weaker believer, then Paul admonishes, you are not acting in love. And that, friends, is the root of the matter; we are to act in love toward those who are weaker. Paul continues:

Anyone who serves Christ in this way is pleasing to God and receives human approval. Let us therefore make every effort to do what leads to peace and to mutual edification. Do not destroy the work of God for the sake of food. All food is clean, but it is wrong for a person to eat anything that causes someone else to stumble. It is better not to eat meat or drink wine or to do anything else that will cause your brother or sister to fall. (Romans 14:18–21)

BELIEVERS *WILL* DISAGREE

As an aside, I understand that for those of us raised in quite legalistic church backgrounds, this is a bit hard to digest. After all, sin is sin, right? If it's wrong for you, it's wrong for me! That's certainly true of the absolutes. But here, Paul teaches that there will be disputable matters, believers will disagree, and some things will be sin for me that are fine for others and vice versa. It's a bit of a shock to the legalistic mindset, but it is true nonetheless.

Serving one another by acting in love as our primary motivator will please God. It's that simple. We must aim for harmony in the church, and seek to build each other up, even through our eating choices; the work of God should not be hindered by food. In fact, it's better not to eat contentious foods at all if it means that a weaker brother or sister is going to stumble. Paul concludes this teaching by giving a summary:

> *We who are strong ought to bear with the failings of the weak and not to please ourselves. Each of us should please our neighbors for their good, to build them up.*   (Romans 15:1–2)

At this point, you might have at least one burning question. You may be asking, *"What in the world does eating meat in the first century have to do with me navigating gray areas in the twenty-first century?!"*

The simple answer is: (A) not very much; and (B) a whole lot.

True, very few (if any) believers today in the Western world would be offended by the meat we eat, although with the rise of veganism, that might well change. However, while we tend to observe the same holy days, such as Christmas and Easter, believers often have differences of opinion on something like Halloween. Should we participate and allow our children to collect some much-desired candy? Or do we understand this practice to be cultish in origin and avoid Halloween at all costs?

All of the sudden, Paul's teaching in Romans 14 becomes *very* relevant. To paraphrase 14:5, "This family considers one day more dangerous than another; that family considers every day alike." Now we're able to work through Paul's teaching:

+ We accept those who disagree without argument.

+ We need to be fully convinced in our own minds about our decision.

+ In all decisions, we must consider the weaker believer and act in love.

As an aside, if dressing up in costumes and letting your kids go trick-or-treating has never been a big deal, you may desire a little more explanation on the observance or avoidance of Halloween. Quite a few Christians have strong feelings about this event. Some see it as a missional opportunity; others as participating in something that celebrates darkness.

Halloween is a contraction of "All Hallows' Eve," the day before All Saints' Day on November 1, as given in the Christian calendar. It was, and should be, a celebratory day for the church.

I personally prefer the redemptive approach to Halloween. Some people remind us that we've redeemed other dates and symbols in centuries past, including December 25 and the placing and decorating of lovely evergreen trees in our homes.

ALL DAYS ARE GOD'S DAYS. THE WHOLE EARTH IS HIS. JUST BECAUSE PAGANS SEIZE UPON A PARTICULAR DAY, AND USE IT TO THEIR ENDS, DOES NOT MEAN IT IS LOST TO THE CHURCH.

Let me be perfectly clear: all days are God's days. The whole earth is His. Just because pagans seize upon a particular day, and use it to their ends, does not mean the day is lost to the church. Some may celebrate evil on October 31; this makes it no less God's day than any other.

Does the modern, popular, incarnation of All Hallows' Eve contain elements that glorify evil and darkness? Yes, of course. Does the modern, popular, incarnation of Christ's Mass—Christmas—contain elements that glorify evil through materialism wrapped up in bright paper with ribbons and bows? Yes, of course.

Must we, as the church, completely avoid events that some will use for nefarious purposes, or may we participate and redeem the day? I prefer redemption.

Halloween is the one day of the year when the mission field comes a-knocking on the doors of Christ's followers. I pray that, despite the darkness others may choose to celebrate, the Christian home will be a place of gracious reception and great light (in both senses), with the biggest and best treats on the street, distributed with a generosity that should be natural to every Christian.

Let children and their parents look forward to their visit to your home. Dress your children in fun costumes, as befits those who redeem. Greet your neighbors. Make the most of every opportunity. Look for God in every moment, for in everyone you meet, the Holy Spirit is already at work!

Back to Romans: so Paul has given us advice on meat (not very applicable in our context perhaps) and the observance of certain days (quite possibly relevant). What about Paul's reference to wine? Well, that continues to be an issue in some Christian circles as we noted earlier, and we'll use it as our example as we work through our next passage.

If you've been following Paul's argument, by now, you may be wondering, "What exactly constitutes a *stumbling block?*" That's a very good question because, after all, Paul is teaching that we must modify our conduct based on whether our weaker brethren in Christ can be offended or encounter a stumbling block from our actions. To get a grip on this concept, we'll turn to Paul's teaching on another incredibly relevant topic, food offered to idols, found in 1 Corinthians 8:1–10.

THE IDOL IS NEVER, *EVER* HUNGRY

Before we begin, it's important to note that Paul's first letter to the Corinthians is what we call an *occasional letter*. Paul is responding to two things:

1. Reports he's heard from Chloe's household (see 1:11) about things happening in the church at Corinth that he's *really* unhappy about. This encompasses chapters 1–4, where he teaches on unity in the face of their divisions; chapter 5, where he has to straighten them out because a man is having sex with his father's wife; and chapter 6, in which he chastises them because Christians have been visiting prostitutes.

2. Questions they have included in a letter to him, saying, for instance, *"Now for the matters you wrote about"* (1 Corinthians 7:1). You'll see the phrase *"Now concerning"* or *"Now about"* at the beginning of chapter 7 (marriage), chapter 8 (food offered to idols), chapter 12 (gifts of the Spirit), and chapter 15 (the return of Christ). These are matters about which the Corinthians

have written to Paul, seeking his guidance. Our question about stumbling falls within this collection of issues.

Now, right from the start, we'll acknowledge that *food offered to idols* doesn't really have a catchy, "This will make me Instagram famous!" ring to it. But much like Paul's teaching in Romans 14, this section of teaching in 1 Corinthians is profoundly useful for navigating the gray areas of the Christian life. Although Paul is dealing with a challenge especially relevant to first century culture—one that still resonates in some parts of the world—the principles he teaches are timeless. There are really two things Paul is addressing: believers who are attending feasts in temples dedicated to idols, and eating foods that have been offered to idols. While the first challenge may be obvious, the second may be a bit murky.

It is customary, even in parts of the world today, to offer food to idols in worship to a particular deity. You may have even observed this in certain restaurants in your community. Now in many cases, those presenting the offering are poor. Day after day, the idol is never hungry (imagine that!), so the valuable food is taken and sold in the marketplace.

This was causing quite a significant issue in first-century Corinth, given that there were both mature believers who realized idols were simply chunks of stone and masonry and newer believers, recently out of idolatry, who were still quite apprehensive of the powers of these false gods. So Paul tells them:

> Now about food sacrificed to idols: We know that "We all possess knowledge." But knowledge puffs up while love builds up. Those who think they know something do not yet know as they ought to know. But whoever loves God is known by God. So then, about eating food sacrificed to idols: We know that "An idol is nothing at all in the world" and that "There is no God but one."
>
> (1 Corinthians 8:1–4)

In these first verses, Paul makes two statements that are going to form the foundation of his teaching on the subject: *"knowledge puffs up while love builds up"* and *"an idol is nothing at all in the world."* He's going to contrast knowledge and love (and the outcome of both), and he notes that idols don't really exist: there's only one God—and He's not an idol.

> *But not everyone possesses this knowledge. Some people are still so accustomed to idols that when they eat sacrificial food they think of it as having been sacrificed to a god, and since their conscience is weak, it is defiled. But food does not bring us near to God; we are no worse if we do not eat, and no better if we do.* (1 Corinthians 8:7–8)

Herein lies the problem: some are so recently out of idolatry that for them, idols still hold a very real and frightening power. They are babes when it comes to following Christ. Paul describes them invariably as having a weak conscience or being weak; this is not in reference to their character, or personal strength, but to the quality of their faith in Christ. It's just so new that it's not had time to properly develop. Paul reintroduces a key concept that's challenging for anyone who has come out of a legalistic church background: *disputable matters.* Just as in Romans 14, he notes that there are things that are sin for some, while perfectly okay for others. And now he comes to the core of his advice:

> *Be careful, however, that the exercise of your rights does not become a stumbling block to the weak. For if someone with a weak conscience sees you, with all your knowledge, eating in an idol's temple, won't that person be emboldened to eat what is sacrificed to idols? So this weak brother or sister, for whom Christ died, is destroyed by your knowledge. When you sin against them in this way and wound their weak conscience, you sin against Christ. Therefore, if what I eat causes my brother or sister to fall into sin, I will never eat meat again, so that I will not cause them to fall.* (1 Corinthians 8:9–13)

That's a mouthful, so let's break it down. Paul mentions their *rights*, almost certainly in reference to the language they used in their letter to him, which has been lost to antiquity. They might have written, "Don't we have the right to eat whatever we want? We're no longer under the Law but under grace!" (Compare 10:23.) True enough, Paul teaches, but be careful that these rights don't become a *stumbling block* to the weak.

PAUL USES THE PHRASE "STUMBLING BLOCK" TO MEAN, "AN OBSTACLE THAT KEEPS SOMEONE FROM SALVATION."

All too often, this has been taken to mean *making the older saints upset*. In my lifetime, and particularly in my parents' time, Christians were often admonished against doing anything outside tradition or the norm, with the firm caution, "You can't do that. You'll offend someone." This, to my mind, was used more to control the behavior of believers than to follow the principles outlined here and in Romans 14. Instead, Paul uses the phrase *"stumbling block"* to mean, "An obstacle that keeps someone from salvation." It's not just tripping them up. It's causing them to stumble in such a profound way that they lose direction, change course, and, ultimately, miss salvation. Paul is telling veteran believers to help those weaker in the faith.

Next, our dear brother Paul uses a bit of sarcasm, one of my favorite Pauline techniques, if I'm being honest. *"If someone with a weak conscience sees you,"* he writes, *"with **all** your knowledge"*—you can almost *hear* Paul's eye roll!—*"eating in an idol's temple, won't that person be emboldened to eat what is sacrificed to idols?"* Worse still, won't they think it's fine for them to also eat food offered to idols and maybe even attend the idol feasts? Then Paul really ups the ante: won't *"this **weak** brother or sister, **for whom Christ died**"* be *"**destroyed** by your knowledge"*? Paul's not playing games here. The mature believer may well have the *right* to eat food offered to idols, but when the weaker brother or sister sees this and copies them, the mature one actually sins, and not just against the weak: *"You sin against*

Christ." Paul is so serious about this that he declares, "*If what I eat causes my brother or sister to fall into sin, **I will never eat meat again**, so that I will not cause them to fall.*"

Paul has now introduced the key principle for this issue as well as this book as a whole: *love limits liberty.* To those who are concerned with their rights, and believe that Christian behavior should be primarily based on what we have the *right* to do, Paul counters with love, unpacking this more completely in chapter 10. But first, Paul uses a personal example from his own ministry:

> *Am I not free? Am I not an apostle? Have I not seen Jesus our Lord? Are you not the result of my work in the Lord? Even though I may not be an apostle to others, surely I am to you! For you are the seal of my apostleship in the Lord. This is my defense to those who sit in judgment on me. Don't we have the right to food and drink? Don't we have the right to take a believing wife along with us, as do the other apostles and the Lord's brothers and Cephas [Peter]? Or is it only I and Barnabas who lack the right to not work for a living?*
>
> (1 Corinthians 9:1–6)

It seems that the Reverend Paul was being judged by those in his congregation! (If you're a pastor, take heart: this type of behavior is thousands of years old—something Moses faced as well.) Paul asks, "Don't we have rights? Don't we have the right to take a wife along with us? Don't we have the right to be fed while we preach the gospel?" In verses 7–10, he gives the examples of soldiers who deserve their pay, and he mentions the Old Testament teaching that even oxen should be able to feed while they are treading out the grain. He continues:

> *If we have sown spiritual seed among you, is it too much if we reap a material harvest from you? If others have this right of support from you, shouldn't we have it all the more? But we did not use this right. On the contrary, we put up with anything rather than hinder the gospel of Christ. Don't you know that those who serve in the temple*

get their food from the temple, and that those who serve at the altar share in what is offered on the altar? In the same way, the Lord has commanded that those who preach the gospel should receive their living from the gospel. But I have not used any of these rights... What then is my reward? Just this: that in preaching the gospel I may offer it free of charge, and so not make full use of my rights as a preacher of the gospel. (1 Corinthians 9:11–15, 18)

By way of personal anecdote, Paul pushes back against those who claim their rights allow them to do anything. Barnabas and I have rights, too, he notes, including the right to make our living by preaching the gospel. But we've intentionally not claimed those rights, he says, so that we may offer the gospel for free. We'd rather work on the side to earn our keep, Paul says. Like all good leaders, Paul first models what he teaches: you can give up your rights for the sake of the gospel because Barnabas and I have already done the same.

After a discussion from Israel's history to help drive the point home, Paul moves in chapter 10 to a discussion on whether believers should join the pagan feasts in the idol temples. On this, he's very clear:

Therefore, my dear friends, flee from idolatry. I speak to sensible people; judge for yourselves what I say. Is not the cup of thanksgiving for which we give thanks a participation in the blood of Christ? And is not the bread that we break a participation in the body of Christ? Because there is one loaf, we, who are many, are one body, for we all share the one loaf. Consider the people of Israel: Do not those who eat the sacrifices participate in the altar? Do I mean then that food sacrificed to an idol is anything, or that an idol is anything? No, but the sacrifices of pagans are offered to demons, not to God, and I do not want you to be participants with demons. You cannot drink the cup of the Lord and the cup of demons too; you cannot have a part in both the Lord's table and the table of demons.

(1 Corinthians 10:14–21)

Paul begins with a command: *"Flee from idolatry."* Using an illustration from the Lord's Supper and from the people of Israel, he notes that those participating in the Eucharist participate with Christ, and those who ate Israel's sacrifices participated in the altar. Although idols are nothing at all, he reminds them, the feasts conducted for them are *"offered to demons,"* and he doesn't want believers to participate with the demonic. One should not celebrate the Lord's Supper, participating with Christ, and also attend idol feasts, celebrating demons. He then returns to eating food offered to idols:

> *"I have the right to do anything," you say—but not everything is beneficial. "I have the right to do anything"—but not everything is constructive. No one should seek their own good, but the good of others.* (Verses 23–24)

Quoting the Corinthians' letter back to them, Paul now gets to the core of his teaching: you might have the right to do anything, but not everything is beneficial or constructive. The goal is never our own good, but rather the good of others. If this principle had been followed faithfully over the centuries of church history, many terrible episodes could have been avoided. Paul then turns to a very practical application of this teaching:

> *Eat anything sold in the meat market without raising questions of conscience, for [quoting Psalm 24:1], "The earth is the Lord's, and everything in it." If an unbeliever invites you to a meal and you want to go, eat whatever is put before you without raising questions of conscience. But if someone says to you, "This has been offered in sacrifice," then do not eat it, both for the sake of the one who told you and for the sake of [that person's] conscience…So whether you eat or drink or whatever you do, do it all for the glory of God. Do not cause anyone to stumble, whether Jews, Greeks or the church of God—even as I try to please everyone in every way.* **For I am not**

> *seeking my own good but the good of many, so that they may be*
> *saved.*   (1 Corinthians 10:25–28, 31–33)

If you're invited out to eat, happily, you're able to do so without inquiring about every dish and wondering, in a very legalistic sense, whether something might have been offered to idols. But if you're told that it has been offered to idols, it's best to refrain, because now, both you and your host are aware, and he may well be watching you to see how you'll proceed. His conscience may be negatively impacted by your decision (verse 29), so it's best to politely abstain. Paul sums up this section by again reminding them of the key principle: do everything for God's glory, not causing anyone to stumble, always seeking the good of others rather than our own good.

 THE KEY PRINCIPLE HERE IS: DO EVERYTHING FOR GOD'S GLORY, NOT CAUSING ANYONE TO STUMBLE, ALWAYS SEEKING THE GOOD OF OTHERS RATHER THAN OUR OWN GOOD.

On this one issue, Paul has both issued an absolute and declared a matter disputable. Attending pagan feasts is an *absolute no* because it's tantamount to idolatry, which is wrong for everyone at all times. On food offered to idols, however, Paul teaches that it may be perfectly fine for some and quite wrong for others. It's a disputable matter, but in everything, the weaker brother or sister must be considered.

BACK TO THE HERE AND NOW

Let's now pull this example into the twenty-first century. For most of us, it probably isn't about eating food offered to idols, or participating in pagan feasts. There are places in the world where this is undoubtedly a concern, but here in the West, it's uncommon. So, to provide a concrete example, let's return to a believer's consumption of alcohol. There are segments of the church for which drinking alcohol of any kind is simply forbidden. Other Christians have happily (and moderately) consumed alcohol regularly without the slightest hesitation.

Paul teaches clearly that there are disputable matters, and social drinking would fit into this category. Drunkenness, not consumption, is the sin, so on this issue, believers will have a variety of beliefs. Some will ask the Holy Spirit our first two questions—"Is this okay for me to do?" and "What are the biblical principles that guide this decision?"—and conclude that they should refrain. But others will feel they have a green light to proceed with moderation. Paul teaches us to ask the third question: "Holy Spirit, by doing this, might I cause someone who is weaker in the faith than I am to copy me and thus do something that is sinful for them?"

Paul's teaching turns things a bit upside down! In some holiness circles, folks would tend to believe that it's the *weak* who consume alcohol because the *strong* are more mature and thus able to refrain. But Paul tells us that everyone must make their own decision about issues like this, being fully convinced in their own minds. As we discovered, you may well feel that under grace, you're quite free to consume alcohol. You may even feel it's your right. But as we learned, *love limits liberty.* So we must ask our third question, and consider whether there are, in fact, weaker brothers and sisters who will be impacted by our actions.

Is it possible that someone who has experienced alcoholism and is trying to abstain would fall back into abuse by observing your casual drink? Then this action, though permissible for you, becomes sin. Might there be younger believers watching you drink at a local bar who will conclude that such a lifestyle is acceptable for them when, in fact, they're not mature enough in the faith to handle the temptations that might arise? This action, though fine for you under grace, becomes sin *for you* because it leads *them* into sin.

Again, this is not about upsetting older, mature saints; they may strongly dislike what you're doing, but in no way are they ever going to copy you. Rather, we must always consider the new believer, the soul who is still immature in the faith, in everything we do. And so we make an effort to follow Paul's advice: *"No one should seek their own good, but only the good of others"* (1 Corinthians 10:24).

This command about seeking *"the good of others"* applies to *all* others, including those who don't yet follow Christ. While we must be careful not to cause our weaker brethren to stumble, we must also thoughtfully consider how our actions are perceived in the world at large and how they may affect our witness in the wider community of unbelievers.

WHO CARES WHAT OTHER PEOPLE THINK?

It seems there are two kinds of people in our world today: those wracked with concern, all day long, over what others think of them and their decisions, and those who don't give two hoots what anyone thinks of anything! In this chapter, we'll seek to strike a balance between the two.

Naturally, as believers, we're called to seek God's kingdom first and always put His will above our own, above the thoughts, dictates, pressure, or even bullying of others. As the apostles declared so clearly, *"We must obey God rather than human beings!"* (Acts 5:29). However, the Bible teaches us that there are situations where we should be very concerned about how we are viewed by others; we are instructed that we must sometimes change our behavior based on their perception.

Perhaps some of us need to pay a little more attention in this area. Then again, I can hear others saying, "But I feel trapped in life because I spend *so much time worrying about what other people think of me!*" I understand; many people, believers included, are almost paralyzed in their life's decisions because they're so fearful that others think poorly of them. Of course, that's not a helpful, healthy, or biblical way to live.

If you're keeping track (and I trust you are), we're now on the fourth question that we should ask the Holy Spirit:

By doing this, might I damage my reputation and witness to Jesus in the larger community outside of the church?

 MANY PEOPLE ARE ALMOST PARALYZED IN THEIR LIFE'S DECISIONS BECAUSE THEY'RE FEARFUL THAT OTHERS THINK POORLY OF THEM. THIS IS NOT A HELPFUL, HEALTHY, OR BIBLICAL WAY TO LIVE.

As a follower of Christ, you've been faced with a decision for which the Bible does not give a clear command or prohibition. You've asked the Holy Spirit whether it's permissible for you, and you feel that under grace, it is indeed. You've sought the various principles of the Word relative to your decision. You've given serious thought, and inquired of the Holy Spirit, as to whether there are weaker brothers and sisters in the faith who might stumble over your participation, and you have determined that the path is clear in that regard.

And so now you need to discover how this decision might impact your witness in the community, among those who do not currently profess faith in Christ. In other words, questions three and four cover sensitivity and consideration given to two groups of people in our lives: those who are following Christ, and those who, at present, would not claim to be Jesus' disciples.

BUT WHO CARES WHAT THEY THINK?

Perhaps you are not convinced that Christians should be all that concerned about culture, or how those in *the world* feel about us. Didn't Jesus warn us that the world would hate us like they hated Him? (See John 15:18.) You may think, "If they're going to hate us anyway, why should we worry what they think of us? Why should we even engage in a conversation with them?"

Good questions. And as with most things in Scripture, a balanced perspective will be helpful. Yes, at times, those in the world will hate us, but that doesn't negate God's command to properly engage culture and concern ourselves with our reputation among those who do not profess Christ.

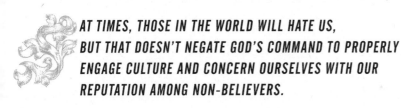

AT TIMES, THOSE IN THE WORLD WILL HATE US, BUT THAT DOESN'T NEGATE GOD'S COMMAND TO PROPERLY ENGAGE CULTURE AND CONCERN OURSELVES WITH OUR REPUTATION AMONG NON-BELIEVERS.

To illustrate this, we'll consider some teaching from both the Old and New Testaments.[10]

SEEK THE GOOD OF THE CITY

Jeremiah 29 provides specific instructions for God's people, who are living in Babylonian exile in a culture that is not immediately welcoming and does not share similar beliefs:

---

10. This section contains edited excerpts from Bradley Truman Noel's *Pentecostalism, Secularism, and Post-Christendom* (Eugene, OR: Wipf & Stock, 2015). Used with permission.

This is what the LORD Almighty, the God of Israel, says to all those I carried into exile from Jerusalem to Babylon: "Build houses and settle down; plant gardens and eat what they produce. Marry and have sons and daughters; find wives for your sons and give your daughters in marriage, so that they too may have sons and daughters. Increase in number there; do not decrease. Also, seek the peace and prosperity of the city to which I have carried you into exile. Pray to the LORD for it, because if it prospers, you too will prosper." Yes, this is what the LORD Almighty, the God of Israel, says: "Do not let the prophets and diviners among you deceive you. Do not listen to the dreams you encourage them to have. They are prophesying lies to you in my name. I have not sent them," declares the LORD.

(Jeremiah 29:4–9)

In the West today, we are witnessing the collapse of Christendom. Ever since the Roman Emperor Constantine announced his conversion to Christianity in AD 313 and unified the empire around the Christian faith, there has been this joining of church and state in Western culture. The heritage of countries such as Great Britain, Canada, and the United States is distinctly Christian, and we owe this, believe it or not, to our roots in the Roman Empire. We have statutory holidays, for example, to observe the birth and death of Christ.

Until recently, shopping was heavily restricted on Sundays, in a nod to the observance of the Lord's Day. For those who may be advanced in years and reminisce about the *good old days*, it can seem like life today for Christians is almost like living in exile; you may feel like a stranger in your own land. The country of your birth has changed profoundly, and the relationship between culture, faith, and state is almost unrecognizable from that of your childhood. The twin pillars of Christendom, church and state, are faltering because in many locales, the state is no longer looking out for the good of the church; in some cases, it seems to be actively (if quietly) in opposition.

Although not everyone agrees, I'm among those who consider this to be a good thing, in general. The kingdom of God was never meant to be tied politically to the kingdoms of this world. While we highly value our democratic freedoms and should certainly engage the political processes of our countries as good citizens, we nonetheless realize that our primary citizenship is in the kingdom of God. And that kingdom certainly does not rely on the fortunes of a particular political party, who sits as a judge in our courts, the persuasion of our elected officials, or legislation currently being tabled! We fully participate, without question, but recognize that Jesus' kingdom *is not of this world* (John 18:36).

In the passage from Jeremiah, we observe God's direct command for His people to settle into the foreign culture, accomplishing everything normally associated with human living, all the while seeking the prosperity and peace of the community in which they found themselves. We see in this letter to the exiles something of Jesus' later description of His disciples as those who are *in*, but not *of*, the world. (See John 17:14–16.) Although the Jewish exiles are to go about their lives and seek the peace and prosperity of their adopted land, they are not to be swayed by the lies of those who suggest that God is acting immediately to remove them from the inhospitable culture.

The parallels to the collapse of Christendom in the West are striking; God will provide both a new perspective and a new understanding of the Christian calling, once our reliance upon the structures of Christendom ceases.

WE ARE THE WORLD'S RED HOT PEPPERS

From Jesus' teaching, I believe we have a clear mandate to engage culture. In the Sermon on the Mount in Matthew 5, Jesus describes believers as both *the salt of the earth* and *the light of the world* (verses 13–14). In Jesus' mind, it is inconceivable that salt can be non-salt, or that light would be hidden or fail to shine. Implicit in Jesus' command to *"let your light shine before others"* (verse 16) is the challenge to engage the darkness, wherever it may be found.

Believers are a crucial component in God's plan of salvation. In word and deed, followers of Christ are to be both salt and light to a decaying world that exists in spiritual darkness. New Testament professor Douglas Hare, in observing the common use of the phrase *"salt of the earth,"* notes it may be difficult for us to grasp the power of its original use:

> We can perhaps catch its force better by substituting another seasoning: "You are red hot pepper for the whole earth!" In this way we are reminded that the statement refers not to status, as if it said "You are the world's ethical elite," but to function: "You must add zest to the life of the whole world."[11]

In a warning to those who would become so *relevant* that they are almost indistinguishable from the world, Hare states:

> Any church that adapts itself so completely to the secular world around it that its distinctive calling is forgotten has rendered itself useless. Its vaunted salt has become tasteless and uninteresting.[12]

Further, and contrary to popular thought, the key point of the Great Commission is not commanding believers to "Go!" but to "make disciples." (See Matthew 28:18–20). How long have we thought it was all about *going*? How long have we thought that only a few of us are called into the missions' field and the rest of us are essentially off the hook? We remain comfortably at home, giving to those who go and praying for them. Unfortunately, this misunderstanding has arisen from some poor translations of the verse in question from the original Greek. In the Great Commission, the imperative or authoritative command is not,

---

11. Douglas R. A. Hare, *Matthew: Interpretation: A Bible Commentary for Teaching and Preaching* (Louisville, KY: Westminster John Knox Press, 2009), 44.
12. Ibid., 45.

"*Therefore go*" but "*make disciples of all nations.*" Literally, we may understand Jesus as saying, "Since you're going out into the world anyway, make disciples wherever you go."

MARS: NOT THE PLANET OR CANDY BAR, BUT THE HILL

The narrative of Paul on Mars Hill (or Areopagus) provides another excellent example of the biblical injunction to engage culture. In Acts 17, we read of Paul's discussion with the people of Athens concerning their worship of "an Unknown God."

Paul then stood up in the meeting of the Areopagus and said: "People of Athens! I see that in every way you are very religious. For as I walked around and looked carefully at your objects of worship, I even found an altar with this inscription: TO AN UNKNOWN GOD. *So you are ignorant of the very thing you worship—and this is what I am going to proclaim to you. The God who made the world and everything in it is the Lord of heaven and earth and does not live in temples built by human hands. And he is not served by human hands, as if he needed anything. Rather, he himself gives everyone life and breath and everything else. From one man he made all the nations, that they should inhabit the whole earth; and he marked out their appointed times in history and the boundaries of their lands. God did this so that they would seek him and perhaps reach out for him and find him, though he is not far from any one of us. 'For in him we live and move and have our being.' As some of your own poets have said, 'We are his offspring.' Therefore since we are God's offspring, we should not think that the divine being is like gold or silver or stone—an image made by human design and skill. In the past God overlooked such ignorance, but now he commands all people everywhere to repent. For he has set a day when he will judge the world with justice by the man he has appointed. He has given proof of this to everyone by raising him from the dead."*

(Acts 17:22–31)

We may quickly observe that Paul was interacting with these individuals in the public square, an open area surrounded by government buildings, businesses, and temples, where citizens could gather to discuss political matters. Paul did not wait for the curious to seek out proper teaching at the Christian place of worship, but he sought an audience with the Athenians on their own turf. Well-trained in the rhetorical styles of his day, and familiar with their Epicurean and Stoic philosophers, he was able to engage these seekers of Athens on their own terms, in a manner readily accessible.

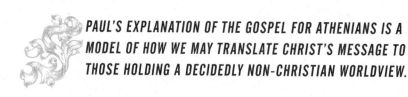

PAUL'S EXPLANATION OF THE GOSPEL FOR ATHENIANS IS A MODEL OF HOW WE MAY TRANSLATE CHRIST'S MESSAGE TO THOSE HOLDING A DECIDEDLY NON-CHRISTIAN WORLDVIEW.

Paul's explanation of the gospel was full of references to their own poets and philosophers; it's a model of how we may translate Christ's message to those holding a decidedly non-Christian worldview. In this Scripture, Paul is an excellent example of how a faithful servant of God can connect with a culture that does not appreciate biblical truths and do so in a way sensitive of others' contributions to our religious and intellectual lives.

ALL THINGS TO ALL PEOPLE

In his first letter to the church at Corinth, Paul describes his efforts to contextualize the good news of Christ:

Though I am free and belong to no one, I have made myself a slave to everyone, to win as many as possible. To the Jews I became like a Jew, to win the Jews. To those under the law I became like one under the law (though I myself am not under the law), so as to win those under the law. To those not having the law I became like one not having the law (though I am not free from God's law but am under Christ's law), so as to win those not having the law. To the weak I became weak, to win the weak. I have become all things to all people so that by all possible means I might save some. I do all this for the sake of the gospel, that I may share in its blessings.

(1 Corinthians 9:19–23)

We should not infer from this that Paul was willing to transform the gospel message into whatever was most palatable to his listeners. New Testament scholar Ben Witherington observes:

> Furthermore, his accommodating behavior has clear limits. He does not say that he became an idolater to idolaters or an adulterer to adulterers. But in matters that he did not see as ethically or theologically essential or implied by the gospel, Paul believed in flexibility.[13]

Paul insisted that his message was simply one of *"Jesus Christ and him crucified"* (1 Corinthians 2:2). He encouraged Timothy to *"Watch your life and doctrine closely"* (1 Timothy 4:16). *"For the time will come when people will not put up with sound doctrine"* (2 Timothy 4:3), but will only listen to that which tickles their fancy.

Indeed, Paul learned how to present the gospel in a manner accessible in a variety of cultural settings, without negating the core of Jesus' message or softening the call to repentance, sacrifice, and death to self. We would do well to model the same, recalling the admonition:

---

13. Ben Witherington III, *Conflict and Community in Corinth: A Socio-Rhetorical Commentary on 1 and 2 Corinthians* (Grand Rapids, MI: Eerdmans, 1995), 213.

Dear friends, although I was very eager to write to you about the salvation we share, I felt compelled to write and urge you to contend for the faith that was once for all entrusted to God's holy people.

(Jude 1:3)

PAGANS ARE WATCHING, SO LIVE GOOD LIVES!

Having established the importance of engaging culture and speaking the truth in love wherever we go, let's consider a verse that really forms the heart of our fourth question:

Live such good lives among the pagans that, though they accuse you of doing wrong, they may see your good deeds and glorify God on the day he visits us.

(1 Peter 2:12)

That's it. Not a long theological treatise, or lengthy passage of Scripture. In just thirty words, Peter gives us a whole lot to think about.

Let's start with the phrase *"though they accuse you of doing wrong."* If you have ever been falsely accused, you may find it comforting to know that long before we ever existed, others experienced exactly the same thing. False accusation, impugning pure motives, and slander in general are as old as the human condition.

Think of poor David, for example, sent by his father to bring supplies to his brothers in King Saul's army. Upon hearing Goliath taunt the warriors of Israel, David asks those near him, *"What will be done for the man who kills this Philistine and removes this disgrace from Israel? Who is this uncircumcised Philistine that he should defy the armies of the living God?"* (1 Samuel 17:26). A perfectly fine question to ask, isn't it? But let's just say that David's oldest brother saw things very differently. Scripture reports:

When Eliab, David's oldest brother, heard him speaking with the men, he burned with anger at him and asked, "Why have you come down here? And with whom did you leave those few sheep in the wilderness? I know how conceited you are and how wicked your heart is; you came down only to watch the battle." "Now what have I done?" said David. "Can't I even speak?" (1 Samuel 17:28–29)

Can't you just hear this exchange between two brothers, especially the oldest and the youngest? Apparently, the nature of sibling relationships hasn't changed that much, even over millennia! David, as we know, was concerned about God's reputation and couldn't believe that this Philistine was permitted to insult *"the living God"* day after day. But his motives were called into question by someone who should have known better.

 IT'S AN UNFORTUNATE FACT OF HUMAN EXISTENCE THAT OFTEN, OUR MOTIVE, OUR DREAM, OUR VISION, OR THE CALL OF GOD ON OUR LIVES IS MOST DIRECTLY CHALLENGED BY THOSE CLOSEST TO US.

As an aside, it's an unfortunate fact of human existence that often, our motive, our dream, our vision, or the call of God on our lives is most directly and powerfully challenged by those closest to us. If only strangers or enemies lobbed false accusations our way or mocked our dreams. Sadly, this isn't always the case. However, *"In all things God works for the good of those who love him"* (Romans 8:28). He has done so many times in the past and will do so again!

Scholars tell us that false accusations were common in Peter's day as well. Did you know that Christians were accused of incest and cannibalism?! Dr. Peter Davids explains:

It was often the very abstaining "from fleshly desires" that caused pagans to despise Christians (so 4:4). They accused them of a number of crimes, such as practising murder, incest, and cannibalism in their secret church meetings (from expressions such as "love feasts," "brother and sister," "eating the body," and "drinking the blood," transferred to pagan contexts), and especially of disturbing the peace and good order of the Empire. Thus [ancient Roman historian] Tacitus claimed that "They were hated because of their vices"…and [ancient Roman historian] Suetonius refers to them as "a class of people animated by a novel and dangerous superstition"…Such slander was the common fare of public discourse and, when brought to the attention of the authorities, became the basis for judicial persecution. Peter knows that nothing can be done to confront this rumor mill directly, for it is a spiteful slander based on the guilt of those who perpetrate it. But, like Jesus, whose words he may echo (cf. Matt. 5:16, where both the "good works" and "give glory" themes appear), Peter argues for a steady course of righteousness that even the pagans will have to approve of in the end.[14]

Peter's very wise advice to those of us who have been accused of wrongdoing—by pagans, friends, enemies, or family—is to live really good lives, and this is how he begins the verse. Now, this isn't rocket science, as they say. Living good lives isn't about following a particular formula, or precise set of rules. This is a simple phrase that Peter likes to use to describe the way of life appropriate for followers of Christ, compared to those who walk in darkness, without the light of God in their lives. Another way to understand Peter's intention in 1 Peter 2:12 is to paraphrase this as, *"Live such godly lives"*—in your speech, your actions, your giving, your lifestyle, your thoughts, and your decisions—that you live as much like Christ as possible. Notice that Peter doesn't urge us

---

14. Peter H. Davids, *The First Epistle of Peter: The New International Commentary on the New Testament* (Grand Rapids, MI: Eerdmans, 1990), 97–98.

to defend ourselves against false accusations, campaign for our *rights*, or seek revenge on those who've hurt us. Not at all. Rather, he suggests that our transformed conduct will be all the evidence needed to acquit us of unfair allegations.

The final phrase ties everything together. As Dr. Davids notes, Peter may well have been thinking of Jesus' words in Matthew 5:16: *"In the same way, let your light shine before others, that they may see your good deeds and glorify your Father in heaven."* Having observed believers living such good lives, those in the community at large—despite their misgivings about the church, and their tendency to falsely accuse—will give glory to God on *"the day he visits us."* Scholars are not certain whether this phrase refers to the final judgment, or possibly the salvation of those previously on the outside. Either way, the outcome is the same: believers living godly lives will bring the proper answer to false accusations and ultimately bring glory to the God of heaven.

As you can undoubtedly tell, this whole concept has particular application to our discussion about living holy lives by grace. Recall our fourth question: *Holy Spirit, by doing this, might I damage my reputation and witness to Jesus in the larger community outside of the church?* What we do or don't do has a particular impact on those watching. While we're clearly to follow the absolutes of Scripture regardless of who objects, whether in the church or not, when it comes to our decisions in the gray areas, we must consider how those watching from the larger community will process our actions. Let's give this concept some practical examples.

WHEN IT COMES TO OUR DECISIONS IN THE GRAY AREAS, WE MUST CONSIDER HOW THOSE WATCHING FROM THE LARGER COMMUNITY WILL PROCESS OUR ACTIONS.

YOU DON'T KNOW JACK

Our fictional Jack lives in a small community with very traditional values. In fact, though a majority of his community would be considered more *adherents* to one of the local denominations than *active participants*, the citizens' morals have been formed by decades of teaching by the local churches—instruction that has often been legalistic in nature, involving the building of more fences than actual laws. In this town, good Christians simply don't get tattoos. After all, as we've noted earlier, the Bible "clearly teaches" that tattoos are sinful. Jack, however, is a decent student of Scripture, recognizes that there are three types of Old Testament law, and knows that the injunction against tattoos no longer applies to believers today. Having dialogued with the indwelling Spirit, he feels that getting a tattoo is certainly something he's permitted to do. He understands from the principles of Scripture that he'll want something that honors Christ, and certainly nothing off-color or lacking in good taste.

Happily, Jack's church has changed a lot in the last twenty years. The old legalistic teaching has given way to a true and proper understanding of grace, and Jack has no worries about causing a weaker brother or sister to stumble. So now he's come to the fourth question and is faced with the fact that while his church has changed, the old teaching and attitudes from decades past still linger strongly in the larger community. While those in the family of faith have little issue with him getting a tattoo, he knows there are those in town who would be honestly disappointed that a Christian has marked their body in a way so contrary to the teaching of Scripture, as they were taught it by the church. So what's he to do?

He asks the Spirit. Is the exercise of his freedom in Christ worth disappointing some of those in the community? Will getting inked resemble Paul's conversation with the Corinthians? *"Yes, all things are permissible, but remember, not all things are beneficial!"* (See 1 Corinthians 6:12.) And note, we're not talking here about whether a Christian getting a tattoo is sinning à la Leviticus 19:28. Rather, we're talking about how obtaining that ink will impact the believer's voice and witness in the larger community.

Yes, Jack is free to get his tattoo of choice…but should he? Is it worth it? You might say, "Well, this is a good chance to show the community that the church has changed. Jack can demonstrate that believers are no longer bound by old legalistic thinking." After all, if the community is still bound by the rules-and-regulations approach to the faith taught by the church of decades past, at some point, now knowing better, we need to admit that this is poor teaching and do some re-education. And what better way to do it than with John 3:16 tattooed clearly across one's body!

Those are certainly points to consider. While you're contemplating that situation, let's ponder another.

TWO SAID NO, TWO SAID YES, AND THREE ABSTAINED

This one is a true story from the early days of my own youth ministry. Just prior to my arrival as youth pastor in my hometown (Mark 6:4 notwithstanding!), the denominational school system that had held sway in our province for five hundred years was replaced by a public system. The Pentecostal schools, which I attended from kindergarten through grade 12, did not have proms. Instead, we had graduation ceremonies, where seniors are celebrated, but certainly not to the extent where dancing is involved! ("We're happy that you graduated, but not so happy that we're about to allow dancing!") Our youth groups tend to have leadership teams composed of teens from the group itself. In the two years between the creation of the public system and my arrival as the newly installed youth pastor, the practice had been that any member of the youth executive team who chose to attend their prom would face immediate dismissal from the team. Just like that. Of course, when I arrived, this was one of the questions I soon faced: if we attend prom, will you kick us off the youth executive team?

I saw in this question a golden opportunity to teach students how to live holy lives by grace. And to be honest, it was from this scenario, way back in 1999, that I developed the questions upon which this book is based. (There were initially only four; the fifth came some years later.) Rather than going the route of Old Testament law and mandating that no student should attend, or alternatively leaving them with no instruction, I gathered my team together and observed that attending a prom falls well outside any command or prohibition given as an absolute of Scripture.

Therefore, we're in a gray area. I outlined the questions and gave them a couple of weeks to pray and talk to the Holy Spirit about the matter. Given how touchy the local church was at the time about our teens attending prom, I then talked with my senior pastor, who, thank the Lord, was incredibly gracious, and waited for their decisions.

THINGS JOHN NEVER SAID

When thou shalt find thyself in thine final year of instruction, be not found attending those celebrations where the lasciviousness of the dancing is apparent to all who walk in the light. Avoid consuming the fruit of the vine in excess. Rather, serving one another in love, make thy presence quietly known, in a gathering of believers in similarly modest dress, eating thy meal quietly and circumspectly. Give thanks to the God of heaven that, having successfully received instruction, thou art empowered finally to leave thy father's house.

Of the seven on my team, two did not get past the first question. They simply didn't feel any release to be able to attend. The Holy Spirit said "No" to their first question. They accepted that with grace. Three others felt it was perfectly fine for them personally to attend, but were very concerned that younger members of the youth group would note their participation and this could be a stumbling block scenario for those weaker in the faith. They therefore elected to abstain. Two of my dear saints, however, got through the first question easily. They noted that while many of their friends would make poor decisions during the festivities, the principles of Scripture would guide them to remain sober and self-controlled at all times. While others may drink to excess, use drugs, or dance in a highly sexual manner, they would not. Further, they felt that their actions would not reflect in a negative manner on those weaker in the faith. Most importantly for this chapter, they had really weighed the impact their decision to attend would have on those in the school at large, who were not members of the youth group. Allow me to paraphrase their response, which I still remember after all these years:

> Pastor Brad, we've thought it over, and we've asked the Holy Spirit the questions you gave us. We feel like we're free to attend, though we'll conduct ourselves in a way that is honoring to God. We don't think there's anything wrong with attending, so we're not worried about junior high students who are watching us, although hopefully they'll ask the same questions of the Holy Spirit that we did. We actually feel that our friend group, including so many unbelievers, needs to see that Christians can attend parties, have fun, and even dance, all the while staying in control and being faithful to who we are. Our friends need to see that we're not boring! They need to see us participating in the life of the school, including prom, and not avoiding everything because we're so *saved*. We really need to do this, not in spite of the fact that we're Christians, but because we are.

With an answer like that, my response was simple: Of course you may attend! Have fun, stay true to your convictions, and congratulations! You're learning how to navigate the gray areas of the faith and life.

Our first story was designed to affirm that these issues can be looked at from diverging perspectives. Should Jack avoid disappointing those in his community? Or should he proceed with obtaining a tattoo, thus helping to reshape the poor teaching of decades past? Jack has to work through that with the Spirit's help. The story of my youth team confirms an important point: different believers will arrive at different conclusions. As Paul indicates when talking about food offered to idols, holy days, or eating meat, there are things believers will face that we may consider *disputable matters*. Christians are not obligated to act in sync, nor should we expect to.

So the lesson from this chapter is that in all things, we must seriously consider how our actions affect and influence those who do not profess faith in Christ. As Peter taught us, we need to live such good lives that even if they're inclined to think poorly of us, they'll eventually see us for the transformed people that we truly are. But before we leave this section and move on to our final question, we need to pause here and ensure that we're proceeding with a clear, balanced perspective.

FEAR OF MAN

It occurs to me that it would be helpful to bring some nuance to this discussion and explore what happens when we get this principle out of balance in our lives. Throughout the last two chapters, we've discussed the importance of being sensitive in our decisions to both our weaker brethren in the household of faith and those in the larger community who are observing our lives.

WHEN IN BALANCE, BEING SENSITIVE TO THE THOUGHTS AND PERCEPTIONS OF OTHERS IS HEALTHY AND BENEFICIAL BOTH FOR US AND THOSE AROUND US.

While some of us need that kind of reminder, others seem almost paralyzed daily as they ponder what others think of them. They find life to be an enormous struggle because every action they take, every decision they make, is clouded by the worry that others will think less of them, whether members of the church or not. When in balance, being sensitive to the thoughts and perceptions of others is healthy and beneficial both for us and those around us. But when it's out of balance, when we are overly concerned about the opinions of others, it becomes a snare to our very souls. We can become so fearful of others' impression of us that we are effectively trapped. I believe Scripture bears this out:

> *Fear of man will prove to be a snare, but whoever trusts in the* Lord *is kept safe.* (Proverbs 29:25)

> *Stop trusting in mere humans, who have but a breath in their nostrils. Why hold them in esteem?* (Isaiah 2:22)

> *So we say with confidence, "The Lord is my helper; I will not be afraid. What can mere mortals do to me?"* (Hebrews 13:6)

> *Am I now trying to win the approval of human beings, or of God? Or am I trying to please people? If I were still trying to please people, I would not be a servant of Christ.* (Galatians 1:10)

> *For the Spirit God gave us does not make us timid, but gives us power, love and self-discipline.* (2 Timothy 1:7)

As you can see, the Bible warns us against getting caught in what's been traditionally known as the "*fear of man*" (or woman). We are, of course, to be quite concerned with the *fear of the Lord*, a phrase meaning the deepest respect for all that God is and submission to His will. We recognize that, as the Bible teaches, "*The fear of the* LORD *is the beginning of wisdom*" (Proverbs 9:10). With grateful hearts, we can submit ourselves to God, recognizing His glory, wisdom, and perfection, being fully convinced that His ways are much higher than ours. (See Isaiah 55:8–9.) Compared to God Almighty, we are but clay in the potter's hands. (See Isaiah 64:8.)

Fearing the Lord and keeping His commandments out of the deepest gratitude and respect for His deity is considerably different than allowing ourselves to be consumed by the opinions of other mortals. So, like many other things in the Christian life, we strive to keep proper perspective: We fear the Lord, but we do not fear people. We are sensitive to the weaker brother and sister in our midst and consider carefully how our actions impact the community that's observing us, but we are not living as people-pleasers, unable to fulfill God's call on our lives because this person or that may be upset, jealous, or generally unsupportive. While we live carefully, we recognize also that people will not always approve or understand when we fully live out the plan God has for us, including the dreams and visions He plants deep within us.

When navigating the gray areas in our lives, we still have one important question to ask that is slightly different than the others. This fifth and final question—"Holy Spirit, is this wise?"—is not so much about sin, but we may need Solomon himself to help us.

7

WHERE'S SOLOMON WHEN YOU NEED HIM?

Here we are, already at the end of our journey! We have worked our way through the first four questions. We've sought guidance from the Holy Spirit on everything from basic permission to move forward to whether our actions might lead a weaker believer astray. We have been mindful that the Bible gives us godly principles by which to make our decisions and guide our actions, and we have recognized that although we should not be governed by a fear of what people think of us, we nonetheless must be cognizant of how both believers and nonbelievers respond to our choices. Our final question involves a critical concept that's rarely discussed these days: wisdom.

To reiterate, here are our questions for the Holy Spirit:

1. Is this right (or wrong) for me to do?

2. What are the principles of the Word that guide my participation?

3. By doing this, might I cause someone who is weaker in the faith than I am to copy me and thus do something that is sinful for them?

4. By doing this, might I damage my reputation and witness to Jesus in the larger community outside of the church?

5. Is this wise?

For a very long time, I taught on this topic using the first four questions in this list. But at a youth conference a number of years ago, I heard my friend Mike Miller teach on wisdom; he clarified that although some things may not be sinful, they certainly may not be wise. In that session, I remember thinking that this would make a great fifth question! And so this final chapter will explore the concept of wisdom, observe how incredibly vital it is in the biblical narrative, and examine very specific teaching on the importance of wisdom in our own lives as we navigate the gray areas of Christian living.

WISDOM: WHERE IT ALL STARTS

It might be helpful to define what we're talking about. In my experience, wisdom is one of those concepts with which we're all familiar, but likely have never deeply considered. In brief, wisdom is the quality of having sound judgment and the ability to think things through clearly, using one's experience, knowledge, and insight to make good, proper decisions. A person with wisdom possesses knowledge of what is right and true, and acts accordingly. The Bible has a great deal to say about wisdom, including where the journey to wisdom begins:

The fear of the LORD is the beginning of wisdom, and knowledge of the Holy One is understanding. (Proverbs 9:10)

There it is, plain as day. The journey to wisdom starts with the fear of the Lord. As we observed in the previous chapter, while fearing the opinion of other people can create a snare for us, we're repeatedly told to fear the Lord. Again, this is not in the sense of *being afraid* of God; rather, it entails viewing God with the utmost of reverence and respect, being fully aware of the differences between Creator God and us, His creation. Recognizing who God is, and who we are relative to God, is the beginning of all wisdom because until we view ourselves properly, in our divinely-ordered place, we will never have the perspective necessary to obtain wisdom.

 RECOGNIZING WHO GOD IS, AND WHO WE ARE RELATIVE TO GOD, IS THE BEGINNING OF ALL WISDOM BECAUSE UNTIL WE VIEW OURSELVES PROPERLY, WE WILL NEVER HAVE THE RIGHT PERSPECTIVE.

GOD'S POINT OF VIEW

As an aside, viewing ourselves as God sees us will automatically keep us from the two extremes that seem to plague humanity: arrogance and poor self-esteem. So much of the world—and the church, unfortunately—lives as though God and His will are far secondary to our own thoughts, opinions, and desires. We so often live for ourselves, proudly believing we are in control of our own destinies. As we've noted earlier, pride is really the root of all sin. As Frank Sinatra sang, "I did it my way"—and my way is better than God's way!

On the other hand, scores of our fellow travellers in this world have an incredibly low view of themselves. Self-esteem issues plague society in general and the church in particular. I'm convinced that many Christians unintentionally short circuit God's plan for their lives simply because *they* don't believe they're capable of the thing to which God has called them. They think, "God could never really be calling *me* to *that*—I'm a mess! I've made more mistakes than anyone I know. I'm a total failure. God only calls people who are successful, who have it all together." Nothing could be further from the truth. The Bible is full of examples of "failures" who became heroes simply because they trusted that the Lord could work through them as He promised.

Fearing the Lord, however, giving due respect and attention to His role in the universe compared to ours, will bring us to a place of healthy balance. We recognize simultaneously that while we are not gods, but merely clay in God's hands, neither are we trash! We are not accidents, nor are we worthless. While on our own we can do very little, we can literally do anything to which God has called us! His strength working in us, via His Spirit, makes us very capable indeed. That's why Paul, who taught plenty about human frailty and weakness, can boldly declare:

I can do everything through Christ, who gives me strength.
(Philippians 4:13 NLT)

We can make the same declaration.

GET WISDOM AT ALL COSTS

Time and again, the Bible teaches us that to seek wisdom, to become wise, is one of the most important things we can do. For example:

Blessed are those who find wisdom, those who gain understanding, for she is more profitable than silver and yields better returns than gold. She is more precious than rubies; nothing you desire can compare with her. Long life is in her right hand; in her left hand are riches and honor. Her ways are pleasant ways, and all her paths are peace. (Proverbs 3:13–17)

How much better to get wisdom than gold, to get insight rather than silver! (Proverbs 16:16)

Listen, my sons, to a father's instruction; pay attention and gain understanding. I give you sound learning, so do not forsake my teaching. For I too was a son to my father, still tender, and cherished by my mother. Then he taught me, and he said to me, "Take hold of my words with all your heart; keep my commands, and you will live. Get wisdom, get understanding; do not forget my words or turn away from them. Do not forsake wisdom, and she will protect you; love her, and she will watch over you. The beginning of wisdom is this: Get wisdom. Though it cost all you have, get understanding. Cherish her, and she will exalt you; embrace her, and she will honor you. She will give you a garland to grace your head and present you with a glorious crown." (Proverbs 4:1–9)

The Proverbs could not be much clearer: we are to get wisdom, at all costs, for it will strengthen and sustain us throughout our lives. Although we chase so many things in this life—power, influence, prestige, material possessions—none can compare with the benefits of wisdom.

If you pause now and think about all of the messages you hear daily about things you *need* or goals that the world says you should seek, so little of it involves the acquisition of wisdom! We can't help but wonder how much of our lives, and our quest for the things of this life, would be made better and richer if we first sought wisdom. There's little doubt the Bible suggests it. As Jesus reminds us, when we seek the kingdom of God and His righteousness first, *"all these things will be given to [us] as well"* (Matthew 6:33).

THE GREATEST WISDOM STORY

Before going any further, let's stop briefly and consider the most famous story of all when it comes to wisdom: the story of Solomon. Even those who have only a passing knowledge of the Bible are familiar with "the wisdom of Solomon." Here's how the Bible records it:

Solomon son of David established himself firmly over his kingdom, for the LORD his God was with him and made him exceedingly great…Solomon went up to the bronze altar before the LORD in the tent of meeting and offered a thousand burnt offerings on it. That night God appeared to Solomon and said to him, "Ask for whatever you want me to give you." Solomon answered God, "You have shown great kindness to David my father and have made me king in his place. Now, LORD God, let your promise to my father David be confirmed, for you have made me king over a people who are as numerous as the dust of the earth. Give me wisdom and knowledge, that I may lead this people, for who is able to govern this great people of yours?" God said to Solomon, "Since this is your heart's desire and you have not asked for wealth, possessions or honor, nor for the death of your enemies, and since you have not asked for a long life but for wisdom and knowledge to govern my people over whom I have made you king, therefore wisdom and knowledge will be given you. And I will also give you wealth, possessions and honor, such as no king who was before you ever had and none after you will have." Then Solomon went to Jerusalem from the high place at Gibeon, from before the tent of meeting. And he reigned over Israel.

(2 Chronicles 1:1, 6–13)

And so, at the very beginning of Solomon's long reign, we see that Jesus' teaching in Matthew 6:33 is indeed true. Solomon sought first God's kingdom and righteousness, and God ensured that *"all these things"* were added to him. God was so impressed that Solomon didn't ask for wealth, a long life, or even revenge! Rather, Solomon demonstrated humility and recognized that without wisdom, he could not possibly hope to reign with success over such a vast population. God granted Solomon's request for wisdom, and Solomon judged difficult matters between individuals (see 1 Kings 3:16–28), gained more wealth than anyone else in the world (see 1 Kings 10:23), and was permitted by God to build His temple (see 1 Kings 5:5).

In fact, Solomon was sought out by a foreign queen, and her words help us bring this chapter into sharp focus.

When the queen of Sheba heard about the fame of Solomon and his relationship to the LORD, she came to test Solomon with hard questions. Arriving at Jerusalem with a very great caravan— with camels carrying spices, large quantities of gold, and precious stones—she came to Solomon and talked with him about all that she had on her mind. Solomon answered all her questions; nothing was too hard for the king to explain to her. When the queen of Sheba saw all the wisdom of Solomon and the palace he had built, the food on his table, the seating of his officials, the attending servants in their robes, his cupbearers, and the burnt offerings he made at the temple of the LORD, she was overwhelmed. She said to the king, "The report I heard in my own country about your achievements and your wisdom is true. But I did not believe these things until I came and saw with my own eyes. Indeed, not even half was told me; in wisdom and wealth you have far exceeded the report I heard. How happy your people must be! How happy your officials, who continually stand before you and hear your wisdom! Praise be to the LORD your God, who has delighted in you and placed you on the throne of Israel. Because of the LORD's eternal love for Israel, he has made you king to maintain justice and righteousness." (1 Kings 10:1–9)

Notice that Solomon's fame had spread far and wide. Even foreign rulers came to seek his advice. Verse 24 tells us, *"The whole world sought audience with Solomon to hear the wisdom God had put in his heart."* Isn't that interesting? Godly wisdom is so attractive and rare that people will travel long distances to hear it.

WISDOM ON SALE NOW!

Hopefully, you're convinced of the importance of wisdom and decide you would like more wisdom than you have. So where do you get some? The Bible points us in the right direction: to God Himself and to others.

For the LORD gives wisdom; from his mouth come knowledge and understanding. (Proverbs 2:6)

In [Christ] are hidden all the treasures of wisdom and knowledge. (Colossians 2:3)

Wisdom is available directly from the God we serve. It's His to give, and He delights in doing so. It's very much like Jesus describes:

Ask and it will be given to you; seek and you will find; knock and the door will be opened to you. For everyone who asks receives; the one who seeks finds; and to the one who knocks, the door will be opened. (Matthew 7:7–8)

But in my experience, what is probably the best-known passage regarding the acquisition of wisdom is one that is frequently misunderstood.

If any of you lacks wisdom, you should ask God, who gives generously to all without finding fault, and it will be given to you.

(James 1:5)

So far, so good. That's not too complicated. We ask, and God graciously provides. Even better, James tells us that God gives generously without finding fault! Now, I don't know about you, but when it comes to God giving gifts to me, His doing so without finding fault is about the only way I'm ever going to receive them! But James doesn't stop there.

But when you ask, you must believe and not doubt, because the one who doubts is like a wave of the sea, blown and tossed by the wind. That person should not expect to receive anything from the Lord. Such a person is double-minded and unstable in all they do.

(James 1:6–8)

Now we see immediately where the trouble lies. Who among us can admit to believing fully, without any doubt? And since almost all of us are in that camp—except those of you who are *reeallly* spiritual!—then we aren't left with much hope. We're apparently like waves, unstable, double-minded, and tossed around. James says specifically that we should expect to receive...nothing. Nada. Zip.

"Wait!" you may be saying. "Didn't James tell us just one verse earlier that God is going to give without finding fault? Seems like all of the sudden, He's all about finding fault because I have a tiny bit of doubt."

After all, if we have to be in a place where we have zero doubt, who is ever going to receive this wisdom that we all so desperately need?

I'm going to say something here that I'm sure you've heard said before, and you probably didn't appreciate it much then either. *What that text means is not what it appears to mean.*

You may protest, "But don't we take the Bible as literally as possible? It says right there, in print, that we who doubt should not expect to receive anything from God!" True enough. We do indeed take the Bible as literally as possible, or at least as literally as it intends us to take it, which would be the subject of another book entirely. The challenge we're having with this passage is more about definitions than a plain reading. If, by chance, *your* understanding of doubt and James' understanding of doubt are not one and the same, then our *plain reading of Scripture* might lead us down some unfortunate paths.

The key to understanding the concept of doubt in this passage is to first understand God's perspective on giving wisdom. There is a scholarly debate about the use of the word "generously" in James 1:5. The word is found multiple times in the New Testament, and it sometimes means "in an excessive way," but other times, it means "simply" or "with single-ness of intention." It's quite possible, given that James focuses upon the person who doubts as being "double-minded," that it's the latter meaning he had intended in this passage. God gives to us single-mindedly, while too often, we who ask are double-minded. God has one intention toward us; we have several in response. There's our first clue in understanding what it means here to doubt.

 GOD GIVES TO US SINGLE-MINDEDLY, WHILE TOO OFTEN, WE WHO ASK ARE DOUBLE-MINDED.

New Testament scholar Scot McKnight tells us that "double-minded" is really the focus of verses 7 and 8. He explains:

The word, literally "two-souled," grows out of Jewish soil, especially Old Testament language of the "double-hearted" person. Daily recital of the Shema [*"Hear, O Israel: The LORD our God, the* LORD *is One"*] makes a "whole heart" devoted to love of God a moral preoccupation, thus setting a divided heart into the context of covenantal [faithfulness] with respect to Torah observance. Also, Jewish [understanding of humanity], as found in Romans 7, frequently understands the human heart as twofold, containing a good impulse...and a bad impulse...But James is less concerned here with the "evil" out-boxing the "good" than he is with a person's heart being split in its allegiance and in the integrity of simply trusting God to provide wisdom. *The double-minded person does not love God wholeheartedly, does not love the neighbor properly, and does not live out the Torah as God intends.* The opposite of the "double-minded" person is the "single-mindedness" of God, which the messianic community is to follow in single-minded trust of God's provisions.[15]

This idea is beneficial in reaching our goal. James is *not* teaching here that believers are to be free from doubt of any kind, or that only those walking in perfect faith can expect to receive from the Lord. Rather, he is warning those to whom he's writing that continually shifting allegiances from God to the world, does not place us in a position to expect God's blessings. We cannot continue to be double-hearted or double-tongued and think God will honor us. Professor David Nystom explains:

Honest intellectual doubts are not in view here. After all, to doubt is human, as the Psalms attest. David, for example, gives voice to his doubts about the character and trustworthiness of God (cf. Ps. 96:1). In Psalm 6 he wonders aloud if God has rejected him, and he even attempts to force God into action by an obvious bribe. Yet in the midst of this honest doubt, David is reminded of all that God has done for him in the past, and he gains the hope necessary to continue. Faith here in James

---

15. Scot McKnight, *The Letter of James: The New International Commentary on the New Testament* (Grand Rapids, MI: Eerdmans, 2011), 91-92. (Italics are Brad Noel's emphasis.)

understands and has experienced the character of God, who gives freely and generously; because of this experience, such a person has confidence. Finally, prayer should be offered in integrity, it should be single-hearted, even as God has integrity and is single-hearted.[16]

The person who constantly waivers in their loyalty to God, who chases one god then the other, is unstable in all their ways. James would have been quite familiar with the tempestuous waves that can arise so quickly on the Sea of Galilee, and he uses this handy local example to describe people who do not follow God with singular intention. They are like the waves of the sea, blown around by every wind that comes along. (Paul uses the same imagery in Ephesians 4:14 in talking about immature Christians.) But the believer who single-mindedly seeks the Lord, who asks for wisdom with a sincere heart, even while entertaining some very human doubts from time to time, can expect the Lord's gracious and single-minded gift of wisdom, without being put under the microscope of judgment. Thanks be to God!

WISDOM UNPACKED

Throughout his letter, James has been combatting false teachers who have promoted themselves as wise, but are producing bitter fruit. Before we move into our final section, we'll pause here and receive additional teaching that is excellent help for our current discussion, and very practical in its application. A couple of chapters after James tells us to ask God for wisdom when we lack it, he writes:

> All kinds of animals, birds, reptiles and sea creatures are being tamed and have been tamed by mankind, but no human being can tame the tongue. It is a restless evil, full of deadly poison. With the tongue we praise our Lord and Father, and with it we curse

---

16. David P. Nystrom, *The NIV Application Commentary: James* (Grand Rapids, MI: Zondervan, 1997), 52–53.

human beings, who have been made in God's likeness. Out of the same mouth come praise and cursing. My brothers and sisters, this should not be. Can both fresh water and salt water flow from the same spring? My brothers and sisters, can a fig tree bear olives, or a grapevine bear figs? Neither can a salt spring produce fresh water.

(James 3:7–12)

You might be reminded of James' discussion in chapter one about being double-minded. He unpacks this a little more for us at this point, with some teaching about the poison that can come from the human tongue, something I'm sure each of us has experienced. Just as salt water and fresh water cannot come out of the same spring, he writes, so too it should be impossible that praise for God and curses for our fellow humans can come from the same mouth and heart. The person who does this is double-minded and unstable in all their ways. This is the kind of person who shouldn't expect to receive too much from God; anyone who regularly disrespects and disparages their friends and neighbors lacks the wisdom we all so desperately need. They may think they have wisdom, but it certainly does not come from God.

Who is wise and understanding among you? Let them show it by their good life, by deeds done in the humility that comes from wisdom. But if you harbor bitter envy and selfish ambition in your hearts, do not boast about it or deny the truth. Such "wisdom" does not come down from heaven but is earthly, unspiritual, demonic. For where you have envy and selfish ambition, there you find disorder and every evil practice. (James 3:13–16)

James apparently is a fan of telling it straight! He pulls no punches here. True wisdom will be demonstrated by good deeds borne out of humility. Bitter envy and selfish ambition, he tells us, is not God's wisdom at all, but *"earthly, unspiritual, demonic."* Can't get much plainer than that. Envy and selfish ambition combine to create disorder, and all manner of evil practice. The apostle definitely has these false teachers in his sights.

The Lord knows we have plenty of disorder and evil practice in our world today as well. This is the world's "wisdom" instead of God's. And as Paul makes abundantly clear, *"The wisdom of this world is foolishness in God's sight"* (1 Corinthians 3:19). The wisdom of the world brings dissension and strife. In contrast:

> *The wisdom from above is first of all pure. It is also peace loving, gentle at all times, and willing to yield to others. It is full of mercy and the fruit of good deeds. It shows no favoritism and is always sincere.* (James 3:17 NLT)

Let's look at each of these in order, for James gives us a wonderful description of God's wisdom and how it should manifest itself in our lives. First, he tells us that wisdom from above is *pure*, without defect. First John 3:3 tells us that those in Christ must *"purify themselves, just as he is pure."* God's wisdom doesn't come with the fresh water and salt water, the blessing and cursing, the single-mindedness of God and the double-mindedness that pervades the so-called wisdom of the world. Next, James tells us that wisdom from above is *peace-loving* and *gentle*. It's not looking to pick fights, promote one's own rights, or argue over the smallest details.

I'm reminded of Paul's admonition in Titus 3:9 to *"avoid foolish controversies and genealogies and arguments and quarrels about the law, because these are unprofitable and useless."* I have to confess: these click-bait headlines we see so often about a believer angrily responding to an argument, or attacking someone with whom they disagree, really get on my nerves. God's wisdom is peaceable and gentle. And, while we're on the topic of the online world, I think we'll all agree that gentleness, even though it is a fruit of the Spirit, is in short supply among Christians. But there's no getting around this; one of the marks of true godly wisdom is gentleness. As Paul reminds us, *"Let your gentleness be evident to all"* (Philippians 4:5).

I'm really appreciative of James' third description: *"willing to yield to others."* Dear Lord, how we need that particular quality today! Our world is so divided, and our conversations are so polarized. Sadly, as you well know, much of this has crept into the body of Christ. We see division over politics, vaccines, immigration, race, gender, sexuality, and almost everything else under the sun. While it's good for us to have informed opinions, and we should know what we believe and why, I fear it's grown increasingly difficult to have an open, respectful conversation that engages those with whom we disagree. The online world certainly hasn't helped matters. As we've noted, keyboard warriors feel free to shout their opinions and insults at people they've never met and will likely never see face to face.

To be sure, there's some good in the online world; we may learn from and engage the expertise of others from around the world. In terms of acquiring knowledge, it's a great time to be alive! But for the believer, all of this discussion, and even debate, must be governed by the simple truth that God's wisdom is manifested in our ability to be reasonable, hearing out the other side, and responding graciously.

The final four descriptions tie everything together. Wisdom from God will be *"full of mercy and the fruit of good deeds,"* showing *"no favoritism"* and always being *"sincere."* It won't seek to lower the rod of judgment at the first available opportunity. Just as God does not give us the treatment or punishment we deserve, so too believers full of wisdom will not seek to bring retribution to bear on those by whom they've been harmed. This wisdom will not grow the bitter fruit of dissension and division, of pride and arrogance. It won't be biased in its approach to others; it will show no partiality. Godly wisdom does not show great honor to the wealthy, while treating the destitute poorly. Favoritism is not a fruit of the Spirit, nor a fruit of wisdom.

Finally, godly wisdom is sincere, genuine, transparent, and honest. It doesn't *put on airs*, or make itself to be something it's not. The fruit of *"the wisdom that comes from heaven"* is abundant: *"Peacemakers who sow in peace reap a harvest of righteousness"* (James 3:18). God's wisdom leads to peace, and the outworking of this peacemaking in our lives reaps for us a great reward.

GOD'S WISDOM LEADS TO PEACE, AND THE OUTWORKING OF THIS PEACEMAKING IN OUR LIVES REAPS FOR US A GREAT REWARD.

WISDOM...AND ALL THAT'S GRAY

Let's shift gears now and look at our final passage of Scripture, one that will really bring the importance of wisdom into focus as we navigate the gray areas of life. Paul writes:

> *Be very careful, then, how you live—not as unwise but as wise, making the most of every opportunity, because the days are evil. Therefore do not be foolish, but understand what the Lord's will is. Do not get drunk on wine, which leads to debauchery. Instead, be filled with the Spirit, speaking to one another with psalms, hymns, and songs from the Spirit.* (Ephesians 5:15–19)

As we noted earlier, people find true wisdom very attractive. They will seek an audience with those known to be wise. That's why the queen of Sheba and *"the whole world sought audience with Solomon to hear the wisdom God had put in his heart"* (1 Kings 10:24).

Despite a great deal of worldly wisdom around us—the self-seeking, divisive kind—there remains a great need for, and desire to encounter, the *"wisdom from above,"* God's own wisdom, given as a generous gift. Those who demonstrate this kind of wisdom may find many demands on their time, for our world (and the church) is in desperate need of the wise counsel of godly women and men.

Paul instructs us to be vigilant as we go about our daily lives. Although we're most interested in the first, Paul is actually giving three contrasts to his admonition:

1. Not as unwise, but as wise

2. Not as foolish, but with understanding

3. Not drunk, but filled with the Spirit

Paul tells us to be very careful how we live—literally, "Watch carefully [or closely] how you walk," with the word "carefully" carrying "the connotation of something done accurately, precisely, or given close attention,"[17] notes New Testament professor Klyne Snodgrass. He writes:

> The call to live wisely is not a call for theoretical knowledge. It is a call for moral discernment and a practical skill in making decisions. The emphasis once again is on the mind and on careful attention to keep life on target, the target being that which pleases Christ and fits his purposes.[18]

We must use and live in godly wisdom, *"making the most of every opportunity, because the days are evil."* Dr. Peter O'Brien makes our purpose clear:

> By using wisdom language the apostle presents the broad sweep of God's redemptive plan, the mystery, for he wants to expand the readers' horizons and encourage them to live in the light of God's declared intentions for the universe. This will have ramifications for all their relationships, with fellow believers in

17. Klyne Snodgrass, *The NIV Application Commentary: Ephesians* (Grand Rapids, MI: Zondervan, 1996), 288.
18. Ibid.

addition to those outside God's people, as the following verse makes clear...Believers will act wisely by snapping up every opportunity that comes. The reason for taking full advantage of every occasion is that the days are evil. These "evil" days are under the control of the prince of the power of the air (Eph. 2:2), who is opposed to God and his purposes. He exercises effective and compelling authority over men and women outside of Christ, keeping them in terrible bondage (2:1–3). But the Ephesian Christians have already participated in the world to come, the powers of the new age have broken in upon them, and they have become "light in the Lord" (5:8). Although they live in the midst of these evil days as they await their final redemption, they are neither to avoid them nor to fear them. *Rather, they are to live wisely, taking advantage of every opportunity in this fallen world to conduct themselves in a manner that is pleasing to God.*[19]

Yes, indeed! As believers, we are to live wisely, as Dr. O'Brien notes, taking advantage of every single opportunity that comes our way. We know, as did the church at Ephesus, that the days are evil. We know we have an enemy who seeks only to *steal, kill, and destroy* our lives and the lives of those around us. (See John 10:10.) We know, as Revelation 12:12 teaches, that Satan *"is filled with fury, because he knows that his time is short."*

In light of this, Peter asks, *"What kind of people ought you to be? You ought to live holy and godly lives"* (2 Peter 3:11).

As we live good and holy lives, we may actively seek opportunities to advance the kingdom of God. Using the wisdom from above, given freely and with single-mindedness, we may pay attention to the culture around us, observe trends within generations, educate ourselves on the topics that are deeply meaningful to those seeking peace for their souls all around us, and prepare ourselves to meet the needs of

---

19. Peter T. O'Brien, *The Letter to the Ephesians: The Pillar New Testament Commentary* (Grand Rapids, MI: Eerdmans, 1999), 382. (Italics are Brad Noel's emphasis.)

our communities. Although the idea of being *relevant* is surely overused, it's safe to say that some churches find themselves in the sorry state of being quite irrelevant to their communities, all the while wondering why they're failing to grow, or are even dying. The great Swiss theologian Karl Barth was quoted as saying, "You should preach with the Bible in one hand, and a newspaper in the other."

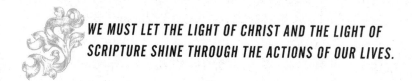

WE MUST LET THE LIGHT OF CHRIST AND THE LIGHT OF SCRIPTURE SHINE THROUGH THE ACTIONS OF OUR LIVES.

I believe this principle fully applies to all believers. We must let the light of Christ and the light of Scripture shine through the actions of our lives. You may have heard it said, "Preach the gospel at all times; if necessary, use words." While it's quite impossible to properly preach without words, the point here is that our whole lives, including our decisions in the gray areas of life, are a testimony to the gospel and the God we serve.

Our lives are our sermons. And as our lives preach these sermons, we must absolutely do so with a cultural awareness of the issues and challenges facing our society. Christians in the West may no longer bury their heads in the sand, isolate from the larger culture, hide in our church buildings, and wait for Jesus to rescue us! No. We must be rather about God's mission, seeking to partner with the Holy Spirit in His ongoing work in our communities. As Alan Hirsch has said, "It's not so much that the church has a mission; it's that the mission of God has a church."[20]

To partner with the Spirit's work all around us, we need wisdom both to discern His movements and to understand the various themes

---

20. Alan Hirsch, "What Is A Missional Church?" Verge Network (www.youtube.com/watch?v=Zv-Hpx-5Ye4, accessed June 27, 2021).

swirling around the public discourse of our times, from racism to social-
ism, from health care to euthanasia, from freedom of expression to
limits on hate speech, from gender and sexuality to politics. Believers
must be informed about the world around them and allow God's
wisdom to enable them to respond reasonably, in a balanced manner, as
befits those who love God with all their minds and love the wisdom that
He freely gives. Acting with wisdom and responding with discernment,
especially over and against overreaction based out of fear and anger, can
be a powerful witness and testimony to lives given wholly to Christ and
His kingdom.

As we seek to navigate the gray areas of the faith, we're faced with
the realization that merely by acting daily in wisdom, our actions can
be a powerful witness to the world around us—a world seeking wisdom
yet not always able to discern the wisdom from above from that below.
It may well be that something is permissible for us, we are mindful of
the principles that guide our decision, and we are sensitive to both the
weaker believer and the one watching from the community.

Yet a decision may still be *unwise at its core*. We may wish to spend
money we don't have on the latest gadget, or upgrade an otherwise perfectly fine vehicle at a considerable loss. We may be inclined to engage
in a particular discussion online, or post certain photos of ourselves and
our lifestyle. None of this may be sin, and none may directly affect those
weaker or those who don't know God. But the act itself may still be
unwise. As Peter has taught us, we can make the most of every opportunity in this world, simply by acting with God's wisdom in all of our decisions. And so, concluding our exploration of the five questions we must
ask when making choices in areas that are gray, we ask directly: "Holy
Spirit, is this wise? Will my action here demonstrate that I'm walking
in God's wisdom? And will I be making the most of every opportunity
toward those outside the family of faith?"

FINAL THOUGHTS

It's been my pleasure to guide you through this topic. I pray that these words of mine, though utterly human, will nonetheless be used by God to bear much fruit for His kingdom as you discern and apply these principles to your life.

Every day, we all face situations to which we must respond…and the knowledge that those responses may or may not advance God's kingdom. Although at first glance some of these decisions seem to have little or nothing to do with God, closer evaluation will lead us to an understanding that as believers, our choices are often more meaningful, and have deeper application, than we may recognize.

My goal in writing this book has been to give believers a tool, a series of questions, by which they can gain insight into living holy lives by grace, confident that they're able to make good and wise decisions. I've sought to share the importance of a relationship with the Holy Spirit, who is instrumental in guiding us through life, and as Jesus said, teaching us all things. I have desired to make us increasingly aware of the effects our choices have upon others, from the weaker sister and brother within the family of faith, to those in the community who are keenly watching our lives. We've been reminded of the significance of differentiating between absolutes and gray areas, and we have learned the importance of employing the various principles given us in the Scriptures. Finally, we've noted that in all things, wisdom continues to be a highly valuable and sought-after commodity in our world. God freely pours out His own wisdom on us, as believers—something for which it's hard to be excessively grateful!

In all things, friends, glorify God. With the Spirit's help, live holy lives by grace, walking in God's commands that are scriptural absolutes and making excellent choices in those areas we understand to be gray. Amen.

ABOUT THE AUTHOR

A native of Newfoundland, Canada, Bradley Truman Noel was ordained by the Pentecostal Assemblies of Newfoundland and Labrador (PAONL) in 2000. He has served as a youth pastor and has taught Bible and theology at the college and university level for more than twenty years.

Since 2008, he has taught at Tyndale University, a Christian school in Toronto, where he serves as chair of the Christian Ministries Department. Brad previously taught at Acadia University, Vanguard College, and Master's College and Seminary, where he created a variety of live and online courses.

He earned his Doctor of Ministry from Acadia University and his Doctor of Theology from the University of South Africa.

Brad and his wife Melinda reside in Springdale, Newfoundland.